The Envelope System

Living Well on $30,000
a Year or Less

By Ellen Zitani, Ph.D.

The Envelope System:
Living Well on $30,000 a Year or Less

By Ellen Zitani, Ph.D.

Published by:
Rebel Hearts Publishing
1309 E Osborne Ave
Tampa, FL 33603

ISBN-10: 0-9972063-3-0
ISBN-13: 978-0-9972063-3-3

Table of Contents

Acknowledgements & Dedication

Many people helped me with this book. Firstly, I'd like to thank my editor at Rebel Hearts, Jimmy Dunson, for his unwavering support. He provided me with very much needed deadlines, constructive criticism and most of all, the encouragement to finish this project. I'd also like to thank the contributors to my case studies. Many of your names have been changed, but you know who you are. It was validating to write your stories, as it reminded me that even though financial stress can feel isolating at times, no one is alone living paycheck to paycheck. Lastly, Dylan Dennehy is the talented young artist who designed the cover. I thank him for his art, his patience and professionalism.

Most significantly, I'd like to thank my mother, Carol Zitani, for teaching me everything that I know about personal finance. The envelope system is her idea, not mine. While I've used this system for twenty years, she has used it for more than forty! I dedicate this book to her.

Introduction

Is this book for you?

My boss loves to talk about how we live in a "VUCA" world; it's volatile, uncertain, changing, and ambiguous. The market is a total crapshoot. Baby Boomers have failed to provide a secure future for Gen Xers and Millennials. Technology and culture now change at a pace unseen by prior generations. And most significantly, the way we define success, failure, employment, unemployment, wealth, and poverty are increasingly more flexible and relative.

People in their twenties, thirties, and forties, meet the challenges of this rocky environment in different ways. Some stick their heads in the sand and do the walk of shame that comes after reckless spending fueled by the "You Only Live Once" mantra. Others take innovative risks which result in either enormous rewards or crucial lessons for the future. But most people struggle to balance their desire for a prescribed version of success and their belief that an alternative path exists.

Whether you are a risk-loving YOLO advocate, a trail-blazing millennial who refuses to be boxed in by a desk job, or just someone who wants some sound advice on the benefits of living moderately, I have one main goal: to teach you how to survive and even thrive on a relatively low wage. Your low wage may be something you've been experiencing for years or even decades. It might be something new for you as your income has recently changed. Or, it might be the bottom line of your very first pay stub. If you want help figuring out how to make the most out of what you have and plan for a better future, then read on.

You may be considering a move to an expensive city for a new job, education, or more opportunities. You may have a twenty-something child or grandchild who is just settling into their new, costly urban life. You might be someone who has been living in New York City, San Francisco, Washington DC, Austin, or any other attractive-yet-pricey metropolitan area and you just need some help figuring out how to make ends meet. You might be someone who had financial security in the past, but now with a new baby, a smaller wage, or after a divorce, you are finding that you need to be more responsible with your money. No matter why you chose this book, you found it. And my intention is to help you think about being smart about your money, regardless of how much or how little you have.

Is this book for wealthier people too? Of course it can be. While I wrote this book for those who live paycheck to paycheck, I can help those with money to spare to live a more moderate lifestyle. Afterall, nobody benefits from gluttonous overspending. Money doesn't make you happy. How you live life does. This book is about subscribing to a moderate lifestyle and why doing so can be one of the healthiest things you do for yourself and your loved ones.

Additionally, this book is about responsibility. But if that sounds too preachy to you, remember that with responsibility comes freedom. I know people usually say the opposite (with freedom comes responsibility), but I think that true freedom comes from being responsible. If you are responsible enough with your finances, then you will find the freedom to do what you want in life. And, if you can be responsible enough so that it feels natural to you, then it won't feel like work or punishment. Instead you will find the freedom that you desire. For you, this might mean the freedom to travel, live where you want, or simply be free from debt. However you define your freedom, then think about how good it will feel when you finally achieve that goal!

I'll give away the bottom line of this book right here in the introduction. My method revolves around knowledge and moderation. Like a good diet, *The Envelope System* is nothing radical or extreme. It was developed years ago by my mother, a working class mom who felt responsible for our family's well being. She knew that her responsibility would give us the freedom to enjoy the best things in life like dance lessons, theater performances and family vacations. Like with a good diet, I intend to convince you in the following chapters that by being a disciple of this method and the various other strategies in this book, you will gradually become far healthier.

Therefore I encourage you to work your way through each chapter. If you want to skip ahead, you'll find the details of the envelope system in Chapter Three, but the system won't work well if you don't first do the work in Chapters One and Two. This book is short for a reason. Any decent advice book needn't be burdensome. My intention is that you will be able to work through this in about two or three hours, then pass it on to a friend. I won't bog you down with unnecessary chatter. I'll get right to the point. I promise. This is about you and your future. In fact, you'll notice handy subtitles throughout each chapter. Use these to determine which sections you need to read and which you can skim.

Why am I an authority on this?

In 2005, I moved from my parent's home in Connecticut to live for the first time in my own apartment in New York City. I had been accepted into a doctorate program in history at the City University of New York Graduate Center (CUNY) and been given a whopping $15,000 annual fellowship. Actually, the conditions of my fellowship stated that I would earn $15,000 the first year, $16,000 the second, and $17,000 the third. I was twenty-seven years old, a bartender with a BA and MA in Gender Studies, I had $7,000 to my name, and a retirement plan worth $20,000. The crucial point in this summary is the date; it was 2005. It was only four years after 9/11, Katrina had just hit, and Americans were completely unaware of what an economic farce the following years were going to be.

The housing bubble burst in 2008, unemployment soared, and in 2012 I graduated with my Ph.D. in History during the worst academic job market anyone can remember.

Yet, you could say I actually picked the best time to be in graduate school. Between 2005 and 2011 four out of my six closest friends who were employed in fields outside of education were laid off; one friend experienced this disappointment twice in one year. Another friend actually experienced the famous Lehman Brothers layoffs. Two friends would foreclose on their homes (one after an expensive divorce), and in my early thirties, I only had one friend who actually paid a mortgage instead of rent.

So while my non-academic friends were straining and stressing in the worlds of finance, law, healthcare, manufacturing, and business, what were my academic friends doing? Were we living the high life? Not at all. Remember the $15,000 fellowship? Well, I considered myself lucky. Some people in my program did not receive any funding while others actually paid tuition to earn their doctorate. And, to add to that sense of luck, CUNY was the only school who offered me any fellowship money at all (out of thirteen applications). So I took the risk, and figured that I would make ends meet some how. After all, I was a decent bartender.

In the fall of 2005 my dad drove a UHaul with my childhood bedroom furniture, my grandmother's kitchen table, my clunky old PC, and my two chihuahuas, to the Queens neighborhood where my grandfather once lived, Astoria. I moved into a 400 square foot studio apartment long before tiny homes were chic. "Who needs a living room?" I thought. My knees touched the tub when I sat on the toilet and my kitchen table was about a foot away from my bed. But I didn't care; it was mine for $900 a month. My New York life had begun.

That fall, I began to quickly burn through my $7,000 in savings. While I didn't have a car, my monthly expenses were more than my $15,000 a year budget would allow. If I continued at this pace, I would be broke by December. So I did what any self-respecting, hard working child of baby boomers would do, I got a second, and then a third job.

The rest of the story will unfold in the chapters of this book. Surviving in a city isn't just about working more. It's about working smarter. I didn't know this at first, but I figured it out eventually. I hope this will help you with your New York (or San Francisco, or Austin, or Portland) story. Living in a city can be costly, but endlessly rewarding. As my best friend Maleeha said, there are opportunities in New York that you just won't find anywhere else. Why not make a go of it? You'll regret it if you don't try. You can do this. You can have your cake and eat it too. You just need a good strategy.

Chapter 1: Yourself

Full disclosure: this is the most painful and tedious part of the book. It is the part where you will have to gather documents like your paystubs, cell phone bills, and bank statements. But when you've completed this chapter, I promise that you will feel empowered because you will have a realistic view of what you have to work with and what your needs are. This is the hard part. This is the real work, but you can do it. Don't skip this chapter. Don't skim it. Do every part of it. And I'm using the word "do" instead of "read" because you will need a pencil and a calculator. One key to success is knowing yourself and the only way to get there is through an honest evaluation. If you feel you need help, buddy up with a trusted friend and do this together.

Trigger warning: you may not like what you learn about yourself. If this turns out to be true, it's okay. Keep reading and I'll teach you to work with what you have.

Happiness warning: you may actually find out that you have more to work with than you thought. If this turns out to be true, it's also okay. The point of this book is to teach you to live moderately, be financially aware, and reach your goals.

So get up off your butt, grab a pencil and a calculator, and get ready to take a good hard look at your assets, liabilities, lifestyle, and growth-potential.

Evaluate your wealth

First, fill out the following charts. Do it right here in the book, or if you plan to re-do these exercises six months from now to mark your progress, first make a photocopy or use a separate piece of paper. Got a pencil? Pay Stubs? Bank statements? Bills? Credit card statements? Good! Now dive in head first. Knowledge is your first step to financial empowerment!

Write your monthly income amount in the column on the right. If nothing, then leave it blank.

Your Monthly Income

Item	Income Amount
Monthly income from job 1	
Monthly income from job 2	
Monthly income from job 3	
Monthly tips or cash earnings	
Monthly income from government sources like disability, social security, TANF, SNAP, unemployment, etc.	
Monthly income from child support	

Monthly income from an ex-spouse / divorce settlement (report if monthly, leave blank if lump sum)	
Monthly income from copyrights or patents you own (mainly for authors and inventors)	
Average monthly income you earn from other sources like renting out a room or selling things you make online or at a local market	
Average monthly income you earn from services you provide (language lessons, tutoring, dog walking, driving for Uber, etc.)	
Estimate the monthly value of any goods you receive in-kind, like free groceries because you cut someone's hair	
Monthly income from a stipend or fellowship	
Monthly income from any other source	
TOTAL Monthly Income	

Look at your total. Is it less than, more than, or right where you expected it to be? If it is more than you expected, then congratulations! If it is right where you expected it to be, then you're already in the right mindset to take full control of your finances. And if it is less than you expected, fear not. The following pages will help you learn to use every cent to its fullest and perhaps even earn a little bit more.

Now that you've evaluated your monthly income sources, let's go through your expenses to see how the totals compare. Fill out the following form and leave the box blank if the expense doesn't apply to you. This is intended for urban dwellers, most of whom rent an apartment. If you are a homeowner, you will have a few more line items, so go ahead and add those items in the blank spaces at the bottom.

Your Monthly Expenses

Item	Amount
Monthly rent / mortgage	
Monthly apartment building or condo fee	
Monthly apartment insurance (insures your possessions inside the apartment)	
Monthly electric	
Monthly gas	
Monthly oil or other heat source	
Monthly car repairs/car	

maintenance	
Monthly water/sewage/trash	
Monthly income taxes (if paid in cash and not through payroll deductions)	
Monthly amount you send/give to family members to support them	
Monthly allowance you give your kid(s) or child-support you pay to their other parent	
Monthly car payment	
Monthly car insurance payment	
Monthly gasoline expenses	
Monthly parking fee	
Monthly public transit pass (subway, bus, etc)	
Monthly carpool / rideshare contribution	
Monthly tollbooth expenses	
Monthly car taxes	
Monthly wifi/internet	
Monthly cable	
Monthly landline phone	

Monthly cell phone	
Monthly data plan for tablets or other devices	
Monthly daycare or babysitter	
Monthly tutoring for yourself or a child	
Monthly out-of-pocket health insurance rate if not deducted from your paycheck. Like insurance from one of the Affordable Care Act/ObamaCare exchanges.	
Monthly prescriptions and monthly co-pays if paid out of pocket and not with an FSA card	
Average monthly groceries*	
Monthly academic tuition for yourself	
Monthly academic tuition for a child	
Monthly gym membership fee	
Monthly student loan payment	
Monthly debt consolidation payment	
Monthly fee for credit monitoring	
Monthly Netflix, Hulu, and/or	

Amazon Prime membership(s)	
Monthly cost for other online subscriptions	
Monthly cost for print magazine and/or print newspaper subscriptions	
Monthly total of breakfast or coffee out*	
Monthly total of lunches or other meals during working hours*	
Monthly total of dinners/drinks out*	
Monthly tuition for dance, martial arts, yoga lessons, etc. for yourself and/or a child	
Monthly cost for salon/barber services	
Monthly cost for tobacco and/or alcohol	
Monthly fee for massage therapy or acupuncture	
Monthly amount for pet food	
Annual vet bills divided by 12	
Other	
TOTAL Monthly Expenses	

* *If you are unsure of the amounts of these expenses, save your receipts for one or two months and then fill in the totals. Accuracy and knowledge are valuable when you are trying to get a handle on your finances. You will also want to do this every six months as your expenses and habits change.*

And now, here is the moment of truth. Fill out these two boxes from the totals of the above two charts:

My Total Monthly Income	My Total Monthly Expenses

If your income is greater than your expenses:

Congratulations! You have a surplus of monthly cash to work with. You're not completely broke. You're not really living beyond your means. Sure, you could probably save some more, but all in all, you're in decent shape. If you do not feel secure in your finances, if you want to learn how to save more, or if your budget does not allow you to sleep well at night, then continue reading in order to learn what else you can do to become financially comfortable.

If your income is less than or equal to your expenses:

You've confirmed your suspicions. There's work to be done, but don't cry. This is just the first step. All knowledge is power, even when it means acknowledging the truth about your personal finances. Knowing what you have and what you regularly spend will give you confidence to make the right decisions in the future.

Evaluate your assets and liabilities

At this point, I encourage you to continue working through this chapter in order to learn about your assets, liabilities, lifestyle choices, and growth-potential. These nuances will play a key role in your decisions about how to live more comfortably, and this knowledge will help you as you work through subsequent chapters. You've already made it through the most difficult part of the book, so have a glass of wine, keep your pencil in hand, and let's take a look at any potential assets and liabilities of which you might not be aware.

Many urban dwellers, especially if they are young and optimistic, may not consider their financial assets and liabilities. What do I mean about this? I mean things like tangible property, copyrights, talents and abilities, and the need for insurance.

Scan questions one through seven and see if they apply to you.

1. Do you own any valuable property or goods?

Some people feel cash-poor when they are actually fairly wealthy in tangible goods. This falls under the category of assets. Do you have any of the following items? Check off the ones you have.

Assets:
- ❏ Rare book collection
- ❏ Record collection
- ❏ Artwork valued over $100
- ❏ Unique/valuable furniture
- ❏ A decent, functioning car
- ❏ A second car
- ❏ Property (real estate) that you do not currently live in
- ❏ An extra, unused bedroom in your apartment or house
- ❏ A futon or extra sofa that is not slept on every night by a roommate
- ❏ Valuable/vintage jewelry
- ❏ Valuable/vintage costumes, clothing, shoes, or accessories
- ❏ Valuable houseware items such as pottery, china, or silver

Make a special note about the items on the above list that you checked off. These can be financial insurance for you to use now or simply for you to sit on. Sometimes we underestimate the power of having something that can help us get through a tight month, or the year when we lost our job. So make note of these now, and know that they will come up in the chapters called "Your Stuff" and "Your Money."

2. Do you own any intellectual property that needs a copyright or patent?

Intellectual property can be annoying to protect in the present, but essential to protect against future loss. If you wrote a book, dissertation, or musical score, or if you have any artwork or inventions that you hope to sell in the future, work toward getting these protected now. The longer you sit on this intellectual property, the more chance you have of watching someone else make money from, or get credit for your idea. These assets will come up again in the chapters called "Your Stuff" and "Your Money."

3. Do you have any physical talents or abilities that need to be insured against loss?

Many people insure their talents and body parts against loss. Athletes, dancers, musicians, and performers all need to consider their bodies to be an asset. For example, pianists can insure their hands. People who work in high risk industries can also insure against injury or disability. If this applies to you, investigate your options this week and consider getting insured against future loss or injury.

4. Will you need life insurance, long term care insurance, or pet insurance?

Children, elderly parents and pets fall under the category of liabilities. Do you have a child or other dependent? Then you should take time this week to evaluate your life insurance policies. Make sure they cover what you would like them to cover. Will they provide security to your dependent in the event of your death? Some people believe that insurance is a waste of money, but others know that it can make a difference in a tragic situation. The choice is yours. This section will discuss the merits and pitfalls of some common forms of insurance. My intent here is not to sell you on a particular idea, but to encourage you to think logically about potential future situations.

Are you worried about the cost of long-term care for yourself or for a parent or loved one? Many people sleep better at night when they purchase long-term care insurance that covers in-home nursing and the fees for retirement/nursing homes. These expenses can shock the uninitiated and the monthly rates often increase with time. But if you, your partner or your parent are approaching the age when you might have concerns about affording care, then take the time this week to consider this as a possible future liability. If you are an adult without children, then this might be a product that can give you a deeper sense of security. In my opinion, if you are younger than fifty, then the lifetime costs of these products do not outweigh the benefits. At the time of this publication, I received a quote for long term care insurance for myself and my thirty two year old fiancé. After doing the math, we decided that we would be far better off if we saved the money we would spend on this type of product because the benefits only last for ten years. But for older individuals, this is a product that can really help.

I'll tell you a quick story. A friend of mine and her wife married later in life. They both had previously been married and they both were approaching retirement age. Their children were grown, and had children of their own to worry about. So the couple decided to purchase long-term care insurance for themselves. My friend and her wife didn't want to burden their adult children or each other if they were to get sick and need care. Three years later, my friend's wife was diagnosed with a condition similar to Parkinson's. The insurance covered her in-home care and allowed the couple to spend a few more precious years at home together. This is invaluable. Long-term care insurance is a fairly niche product on the American market and many people do not even know about it. It may be an asset that can help you stave off a future liability. Like this product, pet insurance also may be something you are considering. Yet unlike long term care insurance, I do not believe that the benefits outweigh the costs.

Many pet owners purchase health insurance for their pet. Average costs are approximately $700-1,000 per year, per pet. However, the average insurance does not usually cover all veterinary expenses. Therefore, at the recommendation of my veterinarian and after a very expensive loss of one of my dogs due to pancreatic failure, I decided to self-insure my other dog by opening a bank account for her.

I deposited $1,000 every year (about $75 monthly from direct deposit). I let the money accrue and it has always been there if I needed it. If my dog is healthy, her annual vet bills are usually around $200 and I save $800. If she gets sick or injured, then I don't have to worry about paying for her care and will never have to make the difficult decision about whether or not I can afford a treatment for her. And after she passes away, if there is still money in her account, I can insure my next dog or use that money for some other purpose. While I think life and long-term care insurance both have merits for some humans, I think pet insurance is a waste of money. For pets, I advocate self-insuring in a separate bank account using direct deposit. Of course, the counter argument for this is that pet insurance and their optional cancer retainers can pay for some very expensive treatments in the event of a serious illness. Obviously the choice is yours. Many people find comfort in these products, even as a means to manage their annual vet bills. But if you have a reasonably priced veterinarian, perhaps opening a bank account for Sparky would be a better long-term choice for you both.

The case studies at the end of this book discuss pets again. If you are trying to live more simply, it is easier to do so without caring for an animal. That said, while I lived in New York City, I had two chihuahuas; one of which is still with me at the printing of this book. I love them so much and they actually encouraged me to be home more so that they would be well cared for. I realize that they were a luxury at a time in my life when luxuries were scarce, but I wouldn't change this for anything. In my twenties, I think about all of the evenings when I made the responsible choice and came home early just for my dogs. Perhaps that mental health benefit alone is priceless. If anything, they saved me from wasting my money out at a bar with my graduate school friends. Walking them encouraged me to get more exercise and to explore parts of my neighborhood that I never would have seen. Because of them, I made a few great friends who also were chihuahua owners! Additionally, pets can ground you and get you through tough times. So it's not impossible to be responsible for an animal (or two!) when you are living paycheck to paycheck. You just have to realize that this luxury comes before any other.

5. Could your unhealthy relationship be causing you some financial strain?

This liability may be harder to measure than others. Are you currently in a relationship that is draining your bank account? This happens all too often to people of all ages. I've seen it multiple times and I've experienced it too. A relationship becomes a financial liability when you find yourself spending more than you can afford in order to promote the relationship. Perhaps your partner has more money than you do and you feel like you need to buy dinner or chip in for theater tickets once in awhile so you don't feel like a moocher. Or perhaps you are with someone who values regular gifts and this has become a custom of the relationship. Most likely, you are just a generous person who likes to treat the one you love, even if that is causing a financial strain on your wallet. In a more serious situation, you may be with someone who is unnecessarily costing you a significant amount of money. I hope it isn't this, but unfortunately, manipulation is as common as it is damaging.

There are only two solutions to this problem: discuss the situation and fix it, or break up. If the situation is not very severe, I suggest having a conversation with your partner. I once dated a woman who was significantly older than me and therefore in a far better place financially. She had just sold an apartment in New York's West Village and had a great job at New York University. Her lifestyle included regular dinners at a trendy farm-to-table restaurant and grocery shopping at an upscale Italian market. After three dates, I sat across from her at dinner and simply stated, "I'm still in graduate school. Your lifestyle is wonderful, but if we are to continue seeing each other, there is no way I can ever offer to pay for a meal at restaurants like this. As long as you are okay with that and understand, I am okay with it. But I don't want you to feel like I'm taking advantage of you." She really appreciated the talk and we agreed that if I ever wanted to contribute, I could, but that I would never be expected to. She understood my situation and while I felt slightly embarrassed at first, after our talk, I never again felt ashamed at the difference in our finances.

A few years later I dated another person who earned approximately four times what I earned. We had a similar conversation, and I thought that the agreement we had reached was fair. Yet as the relationship continued, she repeatedly made comments like: "I'm sick of dating poor girls," or "when do you think you'll earn more money?" Needless to say, this relationship did not work out. Keep an eye out for red flags and know that financial differences can contribute to a mentally abusive situation. If someone doesn't respect you for who you are, regardless of what you have, then that person doesn't deserve to be with you.

I have another friend who is just starting out in life. She is twenty five and has a good job. Many of her friends are still struggling, so she became accustomed to picking up the tab while dating. But just recently, she started dating someone who also has a good job. She remarked how nice it felt to finally share the expenses of dating with someone. So if you are just starting out, know that you are not obligated to always pick up the tab just because you earn more than the person sitting across the table. If you are trying to save, then think about dating like owning a pet. It's a luxury. Be prudent and don't be afraid to cook dinners at home or take a walk around the neighborhood instead of springing for a pricy night out. Meeting for coffee is far less expensive than meeting for dinner. Make choices that you can live with and this will prevent any future resentment in your relationship.

6. Do you have a mental or physical disability, injury or chronic illness?

Disabilities, injuries and illnesses can be considered both an asset and a liability, depending on the situation and the type of assistance you are receiving. If you are currently seeking treatment, then you may qualify not only for disability benefits from the government, but also for housing from your city's housing authority and possibly long or short term disability insurance from your employer. Economically, this qualifies as an asset for you. Do not be ashamed to look into these temporary or permanent options to help you meet your needs. Applications for this type of aid can be daunting; they have multiple hoops through which you'll need to jump, but qualifying may provide you with a more comfortable lifestyle and the ability to focus on the things in your life that are more important than your disease, injury or disability.

Getting the right diagnosis and treatment can help with everything from housing to medication to monthly income. If one of your dependents has an illness, injury or disability, your family may also qualify for some sort of assistance. Seek out a social worker in your community, talk to others who are in a similar situation, and research potential assistance programs. You may have to look through city, county and state websites to find the right program. I have heard of people who have received housing assistance because they were allergic to mold and their current building had a black mold issue. This sounds minor, but I mention it as an example. You have nothing to lose and everything to gain if you investigate your options.

7. Do you live at or below the poverty line?

This book is not intended to be a guide to navigating the labyrinth of public assistance that is available in various cities and states. However, let me indulge you in a personal story. A year after I moved to New York City and became a permanent resident of New York State, I began looking into public assistance programs. I learned that I made $75 per month too much to qualify for free health care. This was an eye opening moment for me as it showed me that my monthly salary really was quite low relative to the city's standards. I never before had contemplated applying for public assistance. But my health care costs were approximately half that of my rent! In the process of seeking aid, which

I eventually did not find (so there really isn't much of a silver lining here), I learned that I might qualify for housing assistance because of the continuous leaks and lack of hot water in my apartment. This story went on for approximately three years and I ended up canceling my application once I found a better job and moved to a less sieve-like apartment. The moral of the story is that it doesn't hurt to try. You may qualify for temporary or permanent healthcare, free or subsidized mental healthcare, subsidized public housing, food assistance or other benefits. Check your city's website and look for a social worker who can provide you with more details. You will need to prepare dozens of papers and therefore become an expert in red tape, but if you qualify, this could help you meet your housing needs so that other aspects of your life will be more comfortable. Imagine if your housing or food needs were met, perhaps you could go back to school or spend more time with your family. Everyone has their own reason for asking for help; don't be ashamed. If you aren't making enough to get by, then see what is out there in terms of help.

Assets and liabilities of all types are often difficult to measure and can be emotionally challenging to contemplate. Everyone has them, so there is no shame in coming to terms with them. Consider your possessions, your family and loved ones, and your future. Think realistically about the possibilities of all of your assets and liabilities and do not ignore them.

Evaluate your lifestyle

You're almost there! Keep that pencil in your hand and work through the next two sections of this chapter. In this section, you will be asked questions about your comfort level regarding possible new income opportunities. Challenge yourself to think out of the box and beyond your usual habits. This next chart will help you evaluate your lifestyle and other possible income sources.

Other Possible Income Sources

Could you...	Your answer (yes or no)
Pick up a second job?	
Ask your boss for a raise or promotion?	
Earn cash weekly by tutoring, walking dogs, shopping for an elderly neighbor, babysitting, cleaning houses, painting, etc?	
Pick up another shift at your current job or switch to a more lucrative shift?	
Rent out a spare room or share yours with a roommate?	

Rent out your futon or couch?	
Sublet your place while you travel or go home on the weekends?	
Make a craft, design lesson plans or can sauces or jellies, and sell them locally or online?	
Regularly find free books, furniture, hardware, tools, etc. that people are discarding and sell them online or locally?	
Ask a family member to give you a monthly stipend?	
Drive for Uber, Lyft or another ride-share company?	
Coach a student athletic team?	
Freelance in graphic design, web design, software engineering, or another tech field?	
Freelance in any other way (personal assistant, personal trainer, life coach, home organizer, decorator, event planner, editor, translator, etc).	
Think of any other way your talents or abilities might earn you some extra cash? If yes, then what?	

The tough thing about living paycheck to paycheck is that we never feel like we earn enough to get by. If this is you, then you need to figure out how to make your assets work for you. I'll tell you a few stories that will hopefully serve as inspiration.

When I lived in New York City, I did all sorts of things to make extra cash. I didn't want to bartend anymore because staying up that late affected my ability to study. But that certainly would have been one way to earn extra income. Instead, I edited books, wrote indexes for academic manuscripts, sold books online, sold hardware online, and rented my futon (and sometimes my bedroom) to travelers. Some months I would make at least half of my rent in supplemental income.

How did I find books to sell? Well, any time I saw "free books" I would pilfer them for anything that looked even half-way valuable. I started a store on a major online book seller, and sold them there. I bought bulk mailers and shipped everything via "media mail" to avoid high postage costs. Some months I made $50 or $100 on book sales alone. Working at a university had its perks. There were free books everywhere. I did not steal any. I found them on tables with a "free" sign, or in a box outside of an apartment building or someone's office.

Speaking of roadside treasures, I used to carry two screwdrivers in my backpack, a phillips and a flat-head. My university was located in a rather posh neighborhood and rich people tend to throw away great stuff. Whenever I saw a dresser with good-quality drawer pulls that someone had put by the side of the road as garbage, I would take the pulls off the drawers and throw them into my backpack. Then I would package this hardware and sell it online. Pulls are very expensive, and a full set can fetch $50-100 or more if you're lucky!

I would do the same with anything I could tote home on the subway that looked fairly valuable. A lamp, a decent rug, an end table, or a painting may be worth something. My friend once found an original piece of contemporary art outside of a dumpster. He had it verified by the artist and learned that it was worth $30,000. She was dismayed that someone had thrown it out; but one man's trash is another man's treasure!

And did I really rent my futon? Of course! It's no big surprise now that sites like Airbnb are making people money hand over fist. Your apartment has equity, even if you pay rent. When I travel, I almost always stay in people's homes and I almost exclusively use Airbnb. But there are many other similar sites like VRBO and Homeaway. I started this while doing dissertation research in Italy. I realized that the same people who hosted me in Rome also wanted to come and vacation in New York. So we would swap apartments. As my comfort hosting in my apartment grew, I opened my door to other travelers and hosted people from around the country and the world. I received $80 per night for my bedroom (I would sleep on my futon) and $50 a night for the futon. If I rented my whole apartment out when I was traveling elsewhere, I would charge $100 per night. This way, every time I traveled I earned money. I had almost nothing of value that anyone would want to steal, and the only bad experience I had was when I sublet to my own cousin who managed to somehow, in only one month, make my toilet and tub look like it hadn't been cleaned in decades. But he was a twenty year old college student, so I forgave him!

Your space is most likely the most precious asset you have. These days, every city and apartment building has different rules about services like Airbnb. When I lived in NYC, I didn't break the laws, and I paid taxes on my income earned from renting my couch and bedroom. Sometimes these rentals earned me at least half of my monthly rent. This also enabled me, for a few years, to live alone instead of having roommates.

This practice comes with both risks and rewards. I hosted travelers from almost every continent and many places in North America. I made some great friends, a few that I still keep in touch with today. Travelers also tend to leave tasty food in your refrigerator. I once hosted a group from Berkeley who came to New York for job interviews. They left me with a spotless apartment and some wonderfully decadent wine and cheese. Another reward was that I learned how to be a good guest by being a good host. I enjoyed the company of the folks I met and never had a problem with any of the folks I didn't meet. Of course there were some awkward moments. For instance, because I offered this Norwegian man dinner upon his arrival, he then asked me what time breakfast would be the next morning. Realizing that he had expectations of future prepared meals, I gently explained that we had great cafes in the neighborhood and that he was welcome to buy food and use the kitchen. The following night he took me to dinner. Now, that's a good guest!

The risks of hosting are myriad. I would recommend that you think about how to vet the people you invite into your home. I asked for contact numbers of current employers or college professors, and I actually called to check up on a few if the guests were not already vetted online through previous stays. I also asked for photocopies of driver's licenses and passports upon arrival to validate identity. Airbnb has a pretty good system of leaving reviews so you have a sense of who is coming into your home. If someone had gushing reviews as a host or a guest, then this made me feel confident. I know that there are nightmare stories out there, but generally the folks who want to travel and stay in people's homes tend to be easy going and in my experience, the benefits of this type of social exchange far outweigh the risks.

Evaluate your growth-potential

Here is where you dream, but dream realistically. I would like you to now evaluate your future. Consider the following questions and jot down the answers right in the book. Put this aside and use it to remind yourself that you are not going to be in the red forever.

1. Look at your answers to the three previous surveys. What did you learn? Do you need another job? Do you have any assets or liabilities that you must keep in mind? Do you have any other possible income sources that you would like to explore? Write them here.

2. Are you currently enrolled in a degree-granting educational program, or do you plan to enroll in school soon? If so, what do you hope to achieve financially as a result of your planned future employment? Be sure to research careers before diving headfirst into one. Learn from me; I had no idea that most academics are broke when I set out to earn a Ph.D. If humanities work was lucrative, I wouldn't be writing this book right now.

3. Do you intend on seeking any professional development or a higher position at your current job that will provide you with more income? Think realistically about the current job market and average salary for the position you seek. When do you think you will reach this position? If you've never thought about this, ask someone who is in your field of work to be a mentor and help you think realistically about what your near future may hold.

4. In five years, where would you like to be? How much money would you like to be earning? Would you like to have a house or car by then? Have you set realistic goals for yourself?

Congratulations! You have completed the self-evaluation section of this book. You might want to keep your pencil handy because there are some fun surveys in the next chapters. Chapter Two will help you think strategically about your stuff. Do you have too much? What do you really need in order to grow into your best self? Then in Chapter Three we will talk about your money. So keep going. You're on your way to financial self-awareness!

Chapter 2: Your Stuff

More than a few years ago, IMG bank had an advertising campaign called "We the Savers." It was aimed at middle class Gen Xers and Millennials who were just starting out and wanted a high interest savings account. But the tagline made me think about everything that I save. And I don't just mean money. Sure, I save money. You'll read all about that in the "Your Money" chapter. But I also save *things*. Sometimes too many things and sometimes too few things. Balance is an art.

In this chapter we will explore what you necessarily and unnecessarily keep. I will try to avoid being prescriptive and preachy. Instead, I will encourage you to evaluate your stuff. What familial or social values are influencing you to hold onto material things and what current desires are influencing you to let go?

There is a whole industry devoted to this topic. Think about television shows like *What Not To Wear* or magazines like *Real Simple*. The most extreme are the exposès on hoarding. These media encourage people to minimize, organize, and be strategic about their stuff. It's not bad advice, but what I'm suggesting is a less sexy and far more moderate approach. You don't need the television-style dramatic make-over. Most likely you just need a slight adjustment to your daily, weekly, and monthly habits.

If we lived in a black and white world, like the one portrayed on TV, there would be only two types of people: hoarders and wasters. Dante had this thought when he wrote the *Inferno* and dedicated an entire level of Hell to these extremes. In Dante's Hell, the wasters were doomed to push a large stone toward the hoarders while shouting: "Why do you hoard?!" Upon receiving the stone, the hoarders would roll the stone back toward their opposites crying, "Why do you waste?!" This unending hellish nightmare is the inspiration for this chapter. You don't want to fall into either category. A healthy balance will make you feel cozy in your space and wanting for very little. So, with an eye toward moderation and avoiding eternal damnation, let's examine your habits.

Hoarding and Wasting

As hoarding and wasting are two extreme ends of a spectrum, let's evaluate where you stand. Use your pencil and honestly mark all that apply:

LIST A:
- ❏ I don't have enough storage space
- ❏ I have to take my garbage/recycling out almost every day
- ❏ I have too many clothes
- ❏ My shoes have a sex life

- ❏ My socks and/or underwear do not fit into one drawer.
- ❏ I have more than ten tee-shirts.
- ❏ I have more than three pairs of jeans.
- ❏ My collection of running shoes could outfit an Olympic track team.
- ❏ There are more than six coffee mugs in my kitchen.
- ❏ I often throw food away.
- ❏ I don't know what's in my refrigerator or freezer.
- ❏ I can't resist a bargain, like buying $20 worth of paper towels just to save $0.10 a roll.
- ❏ I have a hard time fitting the food I buy in my refrigerator/cabinets.
- ❏ I tend to do all of my food shopping at one market because it saves me time.
- ❏ I shop at bulk stores like Sam's or Costco, but I can't leave the store with a bill under $100.
- ❏ I sometimes buy more than one of the same item, especially when it's on sale.
- ❏ I don't know exactly what's in my storage space (or that box in the closet, bin in the garage, etc). I haven't opened it in more than a year.
- ❏ I feel guilty when I throw anything away.
- ❏ I keep an item because I think, "what if I will need this next winter/spring/vacation, etc.?"
- ❏ I accumulate things that I don't really need like hotel soaps, grocery/gift bags, used tin foil, cardboard boxes, or packing materials.

❑ My tupperware cabinet is a mess and I think I have more lids than containers (or vice versa).

❑ My seasonal decorations take up most of the space in my attic, hall closet or storage unit.

❑ I have so many bottles of shampoo, conditioner, lotion, perfume, nail polish, aftershave, and/or hair gel that I could probably not buy any more for a year and still look decent.

❑ I have more books than I have shelving for and most of them I haven't even opened in over three years.

❑ I have enough unused computer equipment that I could probably build a 3-4 desk network.

❑ There is a box of old cell phones and their chargers in the back of my closet.

❑ Yes, there are three broken guitars in the closet. They are right next to the two large vintage suitcases and have been there since my ex moved out.

❑ The clothes in that box on the top shelf of the closet belongs to my cousin who swears he'll pick it up next time he's back home. It's been five years.

❑ There are more than one of each utensil in my kitchen. For example I have four spatchulas and two coffee makers. You know, for when I break one.

LIST B:

- ❑ I haven't bought new shoes or clothes in over a month.
- ❑ I tend to have good quality clothing and shoes that are classic and do not go out of style.
- ❑ I tend to wear each item of my clothing at least once a year.
- ❑ I tend to buy some of my clothing or shoes at second-hand stores like Goodwill or discount stores like TJ Maxx.
- ❑ I donate at least one trash-bag full of clothing and other items to a thrift store at least once a year.
- ❑ I tend to only buy things that I need like food and medicine.
- ❑ I shop for food at multiple stores and markets, because I know where the best prices are.
- ❑ My refrigerator and freezer are neat, organized, and adequately stocked. They are not overflowing, but they are not empty either.
- ❑ I don't tend to throw out food very often and when I do, I feel bad.
- ❑ I only tend to buy the groceries that I need for that evening's dinner, so I tend to go to the market more than once a week.
- ❑ If I find I have a surplus of groceries in my refrigerator, then I make sure not to shop until I've used the fresh food that I have.

- ❑ I regularly use the gadgets and electronics that I have. I tend to donate the outdated ones to friends, charity or second-hand stores.
- ❑ I shop at bulk stores (like Sam's, Costco), but only for staples that I use regularly.
- ❑ I often marvel at the excessive purchases of other shoppers when I am in line at the grocery store. My cart is rarely full.
- ❑ My storage spaces are fairly full, but not overflowing and I know where most things are.
- ❑ When a friend comes to visit, I can easily make space in my closet for her to hang up her coat and shirts.
- ❑ Each plastic container in my kitchen cabinet has its own matching lid.
- ❑ I have a few extra pieces of silverware because those tend to go missing now and then. But I only have enough plates as I have places at my table.

LIST C:
- ❑ I tend to throw out leftover food.
- ❑ I hate eating leftovers.
- ❑ I sometimes regret throwing things away but I know I can always get more.
- ❑ I tend to use things once and get rid of them if I don't like them.
- ❑ I replace decorations, furniture, or other household items before they are broken or

really outdated. I tend to get sick of the things I have and want to replace them.

❏ I always buy the latest electronic gadgets.

❏ I get excited when the latest gadgets are available.

❏ I've waited in line to purchase the latest gadget.

❏ I tend to buy groceries at the closest supermarket or convenience store. I don't have time to go elsewhere.

❏ When I can afford it, I use an online grocery delivery service.

❏ I tend to order take-out or eat in a restaurant more than once a week.

❏ I purge my closets regularly. I give at least two trash bags worth of items to the thrift store at least once a year.

❏ I often will buy clothing, leave the tags on, and then give the clothing away or sell it in a yard sale. Sometimes the new clothing will just sit in my closet with the tags still on.

❏ I tend to buy clothing at full price. I do not have time to look through the racks at discount stores.

❏ I comb the racks of discount stores and often buy more clothing than I need. Shopping is therapy!

❏ I like to buy luxury goods like exercise equipment, lawn furniture, or holiday decorations. But then I will not take good care of them and I will rarely use them.

❑ I tend to throw holiday decorations out after one season. It's easier than putting them away!

❑ I buy so many different things for my cat/dog. They are spoiled!

❑ There are four bottles of olive oil in my pantry.

❑ I had some really expensive truffles in my pantry, but they went bad because I didn't use them.

❑ I've opened my flour container and found mealworms in it.

❑ I have no idea what's in the back of my pantry against the wall. Maybe stuff that belongs to my roommate?

❑ If I'm having a party, I prefer to buy prepared foods from a local market than make my own appetisers.

❑ I just spent $25 on this new hair conditioner that is full of organic botanicals.

❑ When traveling, time is precious. Direct flights only for me.

❑ I have fifteen bottles of nail polish at home, but I get my nails done at the salon once a week.

❑ I often wonder where my money goes.

Meeting Your Basic Needs

As you can probably tell, List A contains habits of people who tend to hoard, List B contains habits of people who have just what they need, and List C contains habits of people who tend to waste. Tally your check marks and ask a friend or roommate if you have been honest. Sometimes we have habits that we cannot clearly see and we can have delusions about the reality of our lifestyles.

I lived in a one-bedroom apartment in Queens, New York for many years. Currently I own a one-bedroom condominium in St. Petersburg, Florida. Both spaces are approximately the same size. When my financial situation improved and I was able to buy a home of my own, I looked for a space that mimicked my New York lifestyle even though I could afford more. Why? Because I realized that living with just what I needed actually afforded me more money, more time, and less aggravation in my life. Trust me, the formula of two adults in a one-bedroom apartment works, even for people who aren't a couple. Here are some tough-love suggestions to help you get your stuff organized and efficient so that you and your partner or roommate(s) can thrive in your small space.

49

Your Kitchen

You have one refrigerator with a built-in freezer. You don't need a second freezer. You want to rotate your food regularly so that things do not go bad or get freezer burn. You should know at all times what you have in your pantry and fridge; so if you have things that are moldy, cruddy, smelly, old, dusty, sticky, or things that you simply know you won't ever eat, get rid of them. Organize your food in a logical way and stick to it. Look at your spices. Do you actually use marjoram or that twelve year old container of paprika? No, you don't. Get rid of them. Make room for the things you use and love.

Get into cooking. Even in cities where groceries tend to be pricey, cooking will save you a lot of money. Seek out the grocery stores and markets where you can buy food at a discount. In my experience Asian, Indian, and Latin American markets have the best deals on staples like produce, rice, spices, oils, tea, and coffee. A one pound bag of Jasmine rice at your local supermarket might run you $4.99 or more. But a ten pound bag of the same rice at an Indian market might cost only $9.99. If you consume a lot of olive oil, be sure to buy it by the gallon, rather than in little bottles. When you cook meals, be sure to cook enough to last at least through lunch and dinner the next day. That meal that cost $10 to cook may provide six meals or more in the end. Try to feed yourself for less than $2 per meal.

If you aren't a vegetarian, then you might want to consider it or at least reduce your meat consumption. Eating meat is expensive. When I lived in New York, I ended up fairly pescatarian by default, simply because it was what I could afford. Think about what you eat and the overall value both to your wallet and your health. Here are some ideas for cheap and tasty meals that will stretch across a few days, are healthy, and are portable (you can pack them for lunch at work). You can look up your own recipes online, but if you write to me, I'd be glad to send you a few.

- Rice and beans
- Pasta with tuna, onions and tomatoes
- Lentils with veggies
- Farro with tomatoes and cod fish
- Whole roasted chicken with root veggies like carrots, parsnips, beets, or onions

If you drink alcohol, you probably already know that having a drink at home is far less expensive than having one in a bar or restaurant. The $5 bottle of wine that you picked up at Trader Joe's will sell for $7 a glass at the bar down the street and $11 a glass at a restaurant. While you spent $9 on a margarita at your cousin's baby shower, your roommate and her friends made a pitcher of margaritas for the same price. And let's face it, she had way more fun than you did. Alcohol is an expensive luxury, but not something you need to give up completely if you're going to live frugally.

Just be wise and avoid buying it in bars and restaurants. If going to a bar is really your thing, put it as a line item in your monthly budget and stick that money in cash in an envelope in your bag (more on this method in a later chapter). When it's gone, it's gone. Don't go using your credit card at the bar. You will literally be pissing your money away.

Money Saving Tips:

- Buy staples in bulk and split them with your roommate(s). That ten pound bag of rice can easily serve you both.
- Ask the local produce seller if they can offer you anything at a discount. Often there will be overripe tomatoes that are perfect for sauce, or fruits that can be frozen for smoothies or consumed that day. In Queens, my favorite produce seller kept a little box in the back for me and another guy named Mario. Anything in that box was only $0.10 per pound if I wanted it. I just had to get to the box before Mario did!
- Ask the bakery if they have any day-old bread. Often this can be purchased for a song and if you reheat it, it will come out like new.
- Seafood generally can be purchased inexpensively at the local markets or Asian markets. If you buy a whole fish, you will spend less per pound, they will probably filet it there for you (you may need to tip the folks

who filet the fish), and you can also take the head, bones and skin to make stock.

- It is less expensive to make your own cold cuts than to buy them. Buy a whole chicken and roast it. Then slice or shred it and use it on sandwiches. You can do the same with a turkey, ham, beef or pork roast. $10 per pound for cold cuts is outrageous. Don't buy them. You can usually get a whole chicken for $5-7. Plus you can use the skin and bones for soup.
- Learn to use different cuts of meat. Yes, short ribs were never expensive until American chefs made them popular. But there are many other cuts of beef, pork, and lamb that are delicious if you cook them right. I'm also a big fan of organ meat. Organic chicken livers cost $2 per pound at my local supermarket. I love to sauté them with anchovies, red wine, onions and garlic then spread them on toast. It makes a wonderful appetizer for a party and the total cost with the bread and anchovies is approximately $6!
- Make your own pet food. Organic and grain-free pet food is expensive. At one point, I spent almost $80 a month on this. So I started making my own, and my dog loves the food I make for her. One batch costs approximately $10 and I feel good because I know exactly what she is eating. In a slow cooker, I combine chicken thighs, livers,

carrots, peas, green beans, rice, and frozen squash. It takes me about five minutes to prepare it and I can cook it overnight or while I'm at work. When I am done, I freeze it into four weekly portions; one batch lasts her a whole month!

Your Bedroom

Most likely you have one closet and one dresser for your clothing. You may or may not share this with a roommate or partner. Look at your clothing. You should only keep things that you have worn within the last year. If you are holding onto that old KISS tee-shirt from high school or that shrunken cashmere sweater that you paid way too much for three winters ago, make like Elsa and *Let It Go*. You won't miss these things. If they are nostalgic, consider putting part of them in a scrapbook. If your underwear and socks number more than ten pairs each, you have too many. They should neatly fit in your drawers, have elastics that still stretch, and they should not have holes. If you have the luxury of boxing up your winter or summer items to make room for this season's, then do so. And use the time when you switch to reevaluate your wardrobe. Practicing this will not only make you feel more organized, but you'll start to realize that you have enough and won't feel the urge to shop for items that you don't need.

I recently made a vow to stop shopping for clothing or shoes for an entire year. I almost made it too. I had to buy some warmer clothing for a winter trip to Canada because I had gained some weight and needed pants that fit me. But I made it from August 1, 2016 - August 1, 2017 without hardly shopping at all. And you know what? I still have items in my closet that I've only worn once! I will keep up this trend through 2018 or until my closet pairs down a little more. I've finally begun letting go of some worn-out items. So go on a shopping fast. See how long you can do it and make a contest of it with your friends or siblings!

Your Bathroom

Your bathroom should contain just what you need. Your shower should have one soap, shampoo, conditioner, and shave gel; it should not have three bottles of shampoo and four body washes accompanied by two old, unwound loofahs. Look at your shower right now. Is it cluttered? Be honest. Now go fix it. If you have roommates, designate one spot in the shower for each person. Strive to have less in the shower than they have. It will be less annoying for the person who has to clean the shower (which is probably you).

Keep boxes in your closet or under your sink that contain one item and one back up. If you have six bottles of nail polish remover, marry them as much as you can, and note that you do not need to buy nail polish remover for the next decade. Use what you have before you buy something new. Knowing what you have and staying organized will help prevent this accumulation of excess stuff and excess spending.

Wasters, now I'm talking to you. Don't go and throw out those five extra bottles of nail polish remover just because you want to get rid of them. Give them to a women's shelter or to a friend who needs them, but don't just throw them away. However, if you do have multiple mascaras or open deodorants (the freshness of which is questionable), toss them without guilt! Keep what you use, and don't buy something if you aren't running out of it. Also, try not to buy products that you won't use daily. You may also want to evaluate the cleaning products under your kitchen or bathroom sink. Go look now. Which do you actually use? Don't be tempted while in the store if you have things at home that you can use up first. Even if you have a cleaning product that you don't like, don't waste it. Use it up, deal with the mediocre job it does, and be sure to never buy it again!

Trimming the Fat

A good friend of mine visited a wealthy friend of his and marveled at his closet. "This man lives in a beautiful, million-dollar condominium. And yet, he has five dress-shirts hanging in his closet! They are beautiful dress-shirts. But he only has five." Yes, less is more. Think about quality over quantity. This will mean different things to different people. It may apply to food for some, clothing or hygiene products for others. You may be someone who prefers organic bath products and so having fewer makes sense because you actually will use what you have. You also may find that you are able to make many of the products that other people buy (like body scrubs or face masks) from scratch. If so, stop buying these luxury goods and make them instead. Or better yet, make them and sell them!

Now living minimally isn't just for the wealthy. Living in a small space and on a small income mandates having less things. Look around you. Can you sell some of your excess? Can you trade it for something else? If you cleared out that corner of your living room where there are four hundred books, could you put in a futon and rent out that space on Airbnb? Your stuff should have a purpose. If it does not, get rid of it.

The motto, "a place for everything and everything in its place" is a good mantra to repeat. Your space should be your sanctuary, while it is also your equity. Use it as wisely as possible. When you truly live the "less is more" lifestyle, you will get more from having less. Remember, with responsibility comes freedom.

Your stuff as an asset

As mentioned previously, your space and your things need to be assets, not liabilities. If you are paying rent on an apartment that is way bigger than you need, then you either need to get more roommates or move. Look at each room, why are you paying rent just to keep your clutter? A storage unit is cheaper than an apartment. My advice: sell your clutter and your space.

My tiny, one-bedroom apartment in Queens cost $1,300 per month at its peak. But I rarely had to pay that amount out of my meager salary. For a few years, I lived with my partner and split the rent. It was during that time that I discovered how to find and sell items on Amazon and Ebay for extra income. As previously discussed, the city was rife with free books, hardware, clothing, furniture, and other items. Once, when my mattress began to rip, I obtained the free, new replacement under its warranty and sold this new one on Craigslist for two thirds of what I had originally paid for it. I took half of that money and bought the generic mattress that I still have today. Every item in your apartment is an asset. Look around and do not undervalue anything you own.

But what if you're just starting out and you don't even have the basic necessities? Well, don't worry. If you live in a city, you'll find things for free. Usually you will meet people who need to get rid of stuff, or you'll see things on the street that you can use. If it is cloth or upholstered, don't take it because it could have bedbugs. But anything that is wood, metal or plastic is safe and you can wipe it down, paint it, or repurpose it. Old boards make great shelves. Old filing cabinets make great end-tables. Discarded crates and wooden pallets are useful materials for shelving, wine racks and even making furniture. And for those of you who are crafty and like to paint, most stores sell "oops" paint at a discounted price. So other people's colorful mistakes can be your super cheap can of amazing hot pink wonder!

Cities also have a way of supplying you with just what you need. Don't go to the department stores for everyday household items. In Queens we had smaller multi-purpose stores that carried everything from dish towels to wine glasses. Almost nothing was more than a dollar or two. But if you are patient enough, you will find the quotidian items for your apartment for free. You can also ask colleagues if they have anything that they could give away. Most people are generally really sympathetic to the "I'm just starting out and I have literally nothing" story. Tell the lady in the next cubicle that you're still eating off of paper plates and she will come in tomorrow with her sister's old set of dishes for you. Trust me. I once went through a breakup and lost most of my pots and pans as a result. I happened to mention this to a colleague and the next day he brought in a whole set of Calphalon for me! He had wanted to replace his old cookware anyway. I was thrilled and those pots and pans were practically brand new! I still use them.

Most apartment buildings also have some sort of message board. If there isn't one, start one. You can post your needs or stuff that you have to sell. At one friend's apartment building, people would leave piles of decent clothing on a table in the lobby. I found the best purple sweater there! Ask your landlord if there is a place where tenants swap usable goods. Or just start one on your own!

Overall your things are an asset. Take good care to have just what you need. The main reason for this is that by eliminating excess want, you'll feel freer. We live in such a commercialized society where we cave to every desire by clicking "purchase" on Amazon. That habit needs to change if you're going to survive on very little. Shopping is not a hobby you can sustain. So be thoughtful about your things and aim to have a use and a designated place for each item in your apartment.

Chapter 3: Your Money

In the last chapter we discussed ways to spend less by minimizing your lifestyle and carefully managing your needs. This chapter will elaborate on some of those topics, but for those on a fixed income, it will also discuss some financial strategies like The Envelope System. Referring to the budget that you outlined in Chapter One will be essential, so make sure you completed those charts. If you skipped that part, go back to Chapter One and complete them, then return here when you are finished.

Earning

Based on the charts you completed from Chapter One, are you earning enough to cover your expenses? The goal of this chapter is to enable you to figure out how to cover your expenses and have a surplus that you can tuck away for a rainy day, or even a vacation! So go back and review what you learned about your situation.

If you are someone who is not earning enough to cover their expenses then you have three options. Option one is to keep doing what you're doing and go further and further into debt. This really isn't an option at all. If you've read this far, I bet you won't let yourself sink into that hole. So then you are left with options two and three. Option two is to earn more and option three is to spend less. Most likely, you will solve your problem with a combination of the two.

Earning more can come in many forms: an extra job, some passive income from renting your space, an occasional rent- or dinner-party, or crowdsourcing a project that you have started. Another sure-fire way to earn more money is to take on an extra job. Many people do this because they like to be able to depend on some income. One of the hardest things about having a lower income but having multiple income sources is never knowing how much you will actually make in a week or a month. This can be frustrating. But this challenge can also be stimulating because sometimes a second job can mean doing something that is a bit outside of your norm. When I was in college and graduate school I worked in restaurants and bars, edited and indexed books, built databases, taught English, and worked in a nursing home. Each of these jobs, while some far more mundane than others, gave me a certain set of skills that I wouldn't have obtained anywhere else. And most of all, they taught me that I can and will find work when I need it.

I also learned something useful, while getting paid in cash can be precarious, it is endlessly satisfying to end a shift with a few hundred dollars in your pocket. I'll never forget the man who would tip me $50 every week simply for serving him his $50 prime rib while he watched the horse races. He'd literally have a glass of water, a piece of meat, watch the races, and then put a $100 bill on the bar and walk out. I still say that was the easiest money I have ever earned.

I am a big advocate of working in restaurants and bars, but I also know that it isn't for everyone. If you land a job at a good restaurant, you can easily take home more than $100 a shift. My best shift earned me $700 in about six hours. Working in restaurants and bars can be tough though. You have to deal with difficult people, you may end up smelling like grease and booze, you'll probably work really late at night, and if you're a woman, you will have to deal with sexual harassment. I don't say that lightly. I've been harassed by bosses, coworkers and most frequently, patrons. The service industry has a lot to learn still from the Me Too movement. But if you need an evening job with good pay, then give it a shot and try working in places where you would be a patron. Start out hostessing or as a barback and test the waters. I know that I'll never be completely broke because I learned how to work in restaurants and thus, I can find work anywhere in the world.

But how can you find employment? Your best bet is to rely on your social network. More people find work through their friends and family members than by looking online. However, in my experience, both options work well. Depending on what you are looking for, you may want to simply ask around, cruise the various internet job sites, or even hang fliers advertising your services. My last attempt in this department proved fruitful. I had to move to my parent's retirement community in Florida because I lost my job. I thought about my new neighbors and their needs. So I made a flier and quickly started a business updating computers, teaching people how to use social media or email, or hooking up their wifi. I also drove people to their doctor's appointments and to the airport, and I even took care of a really cute cat. By the way, cat sitting earned me $70 over four days and the right to use the family's amazing salt-water pool and hottub!

I mentioned rent-parties or dinner parties. This is a really old concept that isn't practiced as much as it should be. A rent party is a party with a cover charge. The host makes a punch bowl of cheap alcohol and provides snacks. Then friends come and bring more friends. Everyone has a good time and if you're lucky, you earn around $50-100. A dinner party is similar, but the concept is perhaps a bit more civilized. It's expensive to go out for a special meal. Think of seasonal foods like lobsters on the July Fourth or a party centered around dumplings, ravioli, sushi or steaks. A restaurant could charge $20-40 for one of those meals. But if you charge $15 per person, you can probably provide the same meal for less and have a little money left over to go toward your rent. You might even know of a budding chef who could prepare the meal as a lesson for your guests. Pop-up restaurants aren't just for the professionals. Of course, flaky people and "bailers" abound, so get folks to pay when they make their reservation. That way, if you're stuck with one hundred leftover ravioli in your tiny kitchen, you made money and you have delicious dinners for the next week!

Anyway, there is no glamour in second, third, or fourth jobs. The reality of our modern life is that most people have to cobble together multiple opportunities just to get by. There is no shame in it and if it helps keep a roof over your head, then it's worth it.

Spending

As I said earlier in this chapter, option three is to spend less. This is the toughest part, especially for people who are accustomed to living a far more cushy lifestyle. So if you are new to living on a fixed budget, then let me lay it on the line for you. If you don't change your spending habits, you will go into (or further into) debt. So controlling your spending means one thing: stick to a budget. Here's how.

First, review your budget. Look at your expenses from Chapter One. After you pay your *fixed* monthly expenses (this means things that are always the same price every month like rent, utilities, tuition, daycare, etc.), how much is left over from your income? Write it below.

Amount left over after monthly expenses are paid: (Line A)_____

Now, assign amounts to the following expense categories:

Category	Monthly Amount
Groceries	
Restaurants/Take-out	
Taxi/Uber/Lyft	
Gas	
Entertainment	
Hair/Nails	
Other	

Next, look in your wallet. Do you see receipts for each of these expenses from last month? Probably not. Most people have no idea what they really spend in a month because they spend their money with a combination of methods: debit card, credit card, and cash. If you are someone who really needs to reign in your spending, then I have the solution: what my mother calls the "envelope system."

The Envelope System

The envelope system comes in various forms: cash (the best form), prepaid credit cards (almost as good), or to monogamously use only one credit card and pay it off monthly. I'll describe the cash system first.

To begin the cash envelope system, you'll need a few envelopes. Label one for each of the categories that you filled out above. If you're really broke, you will need to prioritize your categories. Groceries will hopefully take precedence. This might be the moment you reconsider your nicotine habit or your penchant for cleverly designed bottles of California zinfandel. If you have a bag or backpack that is kept in a secure location and you're not worried about theft, then keep these envelopes in your bag at all times. If you have concern about being mugged, then keep the envelopes at home in a safe place. If you have a car and always go grocery shopping from your car (and car break-ins aren't endemic in your neighborhood) then keep the envelopes in your locked car.

On the same day each month, make a pilgrimage to the ATM machine and take out the amount from Line A in cash. But do not feel rich walking away with that wad of cash in your pocket. You have to distribute that cash into your envelopes. This is your "mad money" for the month. In order to stave off cheating, put your credit card and ATM card inside one of your shoes in your closet. I'm serious.

Hide them but keep them for real emergencies. If you carry them daily, at least for the first month or two while you get used to The Envelope System, you'll be tempted to use them. This will only be cheating yourself.

The beauty of The Envelope System is that you will have an envelope into which you can deposit the receipt for each thing you buy. This will help you plan better for next month as you'll learn the real cost of your purchases. And, if you are a frugal fanny in one category, then you get to move the extra money into another envelope and/or put it toward a more extravagant expense in the future.

Here's an example of what a month on the cash-based envelope system might look like:

Amount from Line A: $200

Category	Monthly Amount
Groceries	$160
Eating Out	$0
Taxi/Uber/Lyft	$0
Alcohol and other vices	$20
Entertainment	$0
Hair/Nails	$20
Other	$0

This was my budget in 2007. This was what my reality was. How did I eat on $40 a week? I was a master of my kitchen. I wasted not and wanted not. I bought fruit and vegetables that were almost too ripe for pennies per pound (see Chapter Two). I lived on beans, rice, and would cook a whole chicken once a week. I bought cheese only when it was half price. I walked to five different stores in my neighborhood just to get the best deals. I never bought anything that wasn't on my list. Shopping like this takes skill, time and willpower. It's a great way to live especially if you don't have a car because you really can't carry too many groceries home. But if you're going to reign in your spending, you will most likely have to start with your groceries and other items on the above chart.

Now, I know getting my nails or hair done seemed extravagant, but I rarely got both done in the same month. Usually I had pedicures in the summer at the cheapest place in the neighborhood, and my haircuts were likewise affordable because I skipped the fancy salon for the locally owned independent shop with fluorescent lighting and no AC. In eight years I only had one bad haircut, so I consider that a success! If you can find friends to help you out with your grooming needs then this would be a way to save yourself some extra money for other goodies. Just recently, my fiancé learned how to cut my hair by watching an online video. He did a great job, the scissors only cost $15 from an online retailer, and

I'm thrilled that I no longer have to pay $30 for a haircut. If you have short hair, you might want to invest in an electric trimmer and ask your roommate to give you that cool fade. Videos can teach you how to cut just about any hair style and even do your own gel nails.

The envelope system really works. Back in 2006, my boyfriend and I saved for an entire year. We were collectively making about $30,000 and we actually managed to save $2,000 for a trip to Key West. I couldn't believe it. We set aside an envelope and just kept putting $20 in there weekly. It grew and grew. Every now and then I'd take it to the bank for safekeeping. When we had enough to buy our plane tickets and made a reservation at a cheap but clean rooming house, we were elated. While on our trip, we used the envelope system every day. We budgeted $100 per day. This seemed extravagant to us, but without a kitchen and on an island where restaurants can be more expensive than those in Manhattan, we knew we'd have to budget high. We spent about $60 the first day on food and then decided that we would save the surplus in a second envelope which we labeled, "mojitos."

Just last year I used the envelope system again while traveling to Norway. I knew that daily necessities like food were notoriously expensive there, so I put approximately $65 a day into an envelope. This forced me to make smart choices every day and avoid "splurging" on anything extraneous. My fiance and I stayed at an airbnb, cooked all but three of our own meals over our two week stay, and had plenty of money for museums and transportation. Because we shopped locally, we still were able to try many Norwegian foods; we even ate reindeer for Christmas dinner! Yes, the irony did not escape us.

Upon our return from the trip, I decided to put myself back on the envelope system so that I could better save for my next trip. I am using a really simple system currently. I take out a fixed amount of cash each Friday at the ATM. This is my money for the week. I put gas and groceries on my credit card and the cash is for anything else. If my dog needs her nails cut, I pay the $10 in cash. If I want a pizza on the weekend, I pay for it in cash. If I want to splurge on something yummy at the farmer's market, once again, I pay in cash. Once the cash is gone, then it's gone. This week I spent approximately $20 on pizza, $25 on Amazon, $15 at the farmer's market, $10 on a glass of wine, and $30 at a bookstore. Next week I will only take out $75 and use the $25 still in my wallet from the Amazon purchase to make up the difference.

My mom used the envelope system for years. She and my dad are children of immigrants; she was a bookkeeper and he was a firefighter. She always managed to have enough for my dance classes, our family trips to the theater, and regular camping trips in our pick-up truck. My mom is a wiz with accounting and this system is not my own, but hers. It works. She is living proof. Right now, she has six bank envelopes labeled hair, eggs from the farmer, fun, veggies from the farmer's market, quilting supplies, and new sneakers. She even has an envelope that she gives to my dad each month, which is his "allowance"!

I mentioned that there were two other ways to use the envelope system, by using a prepaid credit card or monogamously using a credit card. A prepaid credit card works almost as well as cash, and you can put the receipts from any transaction with a credit, debit, or prepaid card into an appropriately labeled envelope. I would also keep a tally on the outside of the envelope of how much you've spent so that a quick glance at your envelopes will tell you where you are this month and help you determine if you can make that purchase you are contemplating.

One time, my roommate and I decided that we were spending too much on groceries. We didn't have a shared bank account and were basically just buying our own things and sharing regularly. I had a feeling that we both were overbuying, so I asked him to put each grocery receipt on the refrigerator under a magnet. At the end of the month I added up the total from the receipts and itemized the expenses into categories. In addition to realizing that we collectively spent approximately $40 on bacon, it was clear that we had overspent. We banned bacon, chicharon, and snack food from our grocery bills. We also decided that we would buy frozen spinach and frozen veggies when palatable, because we had spent oodles on those plastic boxes of organic greens. After two months with these new rules, our collective grocery bills were 20% lower. We also had the camaraderie of being more frugal together and would brag to each about bargains we found.

Finally, the electronic form of the envelope system will enable you to easily save for a vacation or anything else. As I mentioned, the easiest way is to stash cash away in a safe space. But once, I decided to save for a vacation with another person. We made a budget of our expenses and estimated how much it would cost. Then we contributed the same amount to a vacation account in a bank each month. The money grew fast and our budget enabled us to go away for an entire month. While on vacation, we used the envelope system to manage our daily budget just as I had done in Key West. We had envelopes for food, transportation, and souvenirs. Plus, because the vacation was completely paid for prior to our departure, the money I earned from my salaried job while I was away continued to be deposited into my bank account. When I returned, because I didn't spend any money on gas or groceries for a month, I came home to a surplus!

Saving

Effective saving requires a budget just as responsible spending does. If you revisit the chart in the "Spending" section of this chapter and add a line, "saving for _____," this is most likely the easiest way to save for almost anything. Maybe you know you're going to need a new computer in a few months. Maybe the holidays are coming up and you want to plan ahead. Maybe you want to go away and have enough for the ticket, but need to budget for your daily spending-money for your trip. Maybe you're starting school and will need books. There are a ton of things we need to save for. And if we do so effectively, we won't feel the pinch as much when the expense arrives. Because there are so many ways to save money, I've put them into a bulleted list below:

- **Open a separate bank account.** Many savings accounts come with no annual fee and no minimum deposit. You can use direct deposit or your phone to transfer money from your paycheck or your checking account into your savings account. I recommend not having a checkbook or an ATM card for this account. In other words, open a savings account at a bank where you do not already do business. The only way you could get funds is through a transfer or a withdrawal in person. This will discourage cheating. This also is a great way to save with someone else to whom you are not financially tied. You both can deposit the same amount regularly, jointly own it, and watch it grow. Always know that if they are a jerk, they may take off with the balance. So make your decisions wisely and don't spend time with jerks.

- **Use the envelope system.** This works well for saving smaller sums of money. Maybe you owe your sister $200, or you know you're going to need some car repairs soon. I don't recommend saving more than $500 in an envelope, simply because cash can be lost or stolen. But having an envelope provides you with a tangible reminder of your goal.
- **Have a relative help you.** If you are close to a parent or sibling who is very responsible, perhaps they can hold the money for you. If you really don't trust yourself, then asking someone else who is more trustworthy will work. It will make you accountable to someone else, and you'll feel satisfied knowing that you are working toward your goal.
- **Pay yourself in installments.** Sometimes if there is something you want, you can pay yourself in installments. Perhaps you need a new laptop and plan to spend $500 on it. Let's say you have $200. You can put that aside in an envelope or in a separate account and add to it when you can. Or you could buy a prepaid credit card with the cash and stash that card somewhere safe. When you have another $100, then you do the same, until you reach $500. The important thing is to wait until you can afford the item before buying it. Sometimes, especially with items like computers or cell phones, we feel like we cannot survive without them. Be creative. In

the meantime, use public computers or the ones at your school, or borrow one from a friend or relative. Don't go into debt; it's not worth it. Wait until you've saved enough money to buy what you need and that way you will only buy what you can truly afford.

- **If you have a partner, live off of one income.** I know it sounds nuts, but if there are two of you and you are very much committed, why not try to live off of one income and save the other? My grandparents did this. My grandmother worked for a jet engine manufacturing company and my grandfather built railroad bridges. Well into retirement, they would take entire pension checks and put them away. They lived off of my grandmother's retirement for years while saving both of their social security checks and my grandfather's retirement income. Frugality works well. If you both work toward the goal and you can pair down your expenses enough, then living off of one income can be one of the most effective means of saving that exists for working-class people.

Saving money pays off in the long run. While in my thirties, I lived with my parents for a while in order to save money for a down-payment on my very first home. This dream seemed lofty to me for a long time, but when the real estate market took a turn for the worse, I saw this as my opportunity. I am currently a high school teacher, so I don't make a lot of money. But living with my parents for almost two years while I worked full time helped me save more than half of my salary.

I currently have three bank accounts. One is for checking, one is for savings (and it's located in another state!) and one is for long-term retirement. My mother always said, "pay yourself first." I contribute the maximum allowed to my retirement account, and I live off of a strict budget that equals the amount deposited into my checking account monthly after approximately 25% of my salary is deposited into a savings account at an out-of-state bank. Even after purchasing my condo, I still use this method, and made sure to buy a condo that I could afford on approximately 60% of my salary. I didn't want to change my savings habit. I had the opportunity to purchase a far more expensive condo, which was a very good value. But I chose a smaller condo that was in good condition and at a very low price. My mortgage is cheaper than my car payment was; I sleep very well every night knowing this. I expect to be able to pay it off after five years.

The next chapter is about your future. Most people contemplate their future in some way every day. Whether this causes you anxiety or hope will depend on what you are doing now to control it.

Chapter 4: Your Future

Let's face it. The future is scary. It's an unknown wilderness of history yet to be told. Yet, the perpetual hope for a better tomorrow seems somehow ingrained in the human psychological condition. But despite humanity's unexplainable optimistic lens, when we think about our individual financial futures, many of us shrug in wonder at the unknown.

When I lived in New York City, I used to attend a queer Buddhist sangha. My takeaway from these Sunday night meditation sessions was that we have control over some things in life and we do not have control over other things. We cannot control other people, and we cannot control reactions to situations that are beyond our control. But we can control our own choices, and in many cases that includes how we choose to react. So, while we cannot control the future, we can control some of our reactions to present or past events. And this makes the future less scary. The main point is to learn from our mistakes.

Let me provide an example. I only have two major regrets in my life, neither of which was financial. One was not attending a certain graduate program when I had the chance and the second was getting into a car with a drunk driver. Both situations gratefully turned out just fine. I survived that ride, and so did everyone else. But I knew it was a stupid decision at the time and I regret it to this day.

Regarding graduate school, I ended up in a different program a few years later, so all was not lost.

What do you do when you have a financial regret? You do the same thing you do when you have a life-lesson regret. You learn from it. My most recent major purchase, aside from my condo, was my car. Two weeks after I began work at my current job, I stopped at an auto dealership to test drive cars because I was driving my mother's SUV and I felt like I needed my own car. I hastily (making a dozen or so textbook mistakes along the way) purchased a brand new car and overpaid by approximately $3,000. And while I regret this, I also learned from it.

With this experience, I learned to:

- trust my gut
- ignore others who think they know what they are talking about
- be prepared to negotiate when making a major purchase
- only make a major purchase when I'm not feeling emotional, especially if that emotion is excitement
- not buy a black car in Florida.

But this chapter is about your future, not your mistakes. So what do mistakes have to do with your future? Well, they mold you into the person you are. Every mistake, no matter how vast (such as incredible debt, impulse spending, overspending, or living beyond your means) serves as a weapon in your arsenal against future bad decisions. You may have felt out of control then, but now you can control how you use your knowledge to your advantage. How you think about your future will play a large role in determining its outcome.

Growth

In many ways, this book is about perspective. If you are looking at your past and thinking that you were a financial trainwreck, then you are already changing your perspective. If you are still a complete trainwreck but are holding fast to your fancy cupcake habit or your desire for those $200 Cole Haan shoes, then your perspective has not yet changed. But you did pick up this book for some reason. And that, my friend, is the light at the end of your trainwreck tunnel. You know you need to change your perspective. But how?

Look around you. Who are the people in your life who seem to have it together? Look at the people in your social network who travel, who have clean and attractive living spaces, and who seem fulfilled in their jobs. Chances are, you may feel envy when you gaze longingly at their honeymoon pictures or visit their Ikea-perfect apartment. We all know that appearances are not always indicative of the truth, but we also know that this book is about you, not them. So here's what to do.

Check your envy. Notice it. Look at it. What is it that you really envy? Is it a simpler life? Is it more stuff? Is it a more aesthetically pleasing space? Is it the financial security? Is it the ability to travel? Now take out a pen and write down what it is that you admire or envy about the apparent lifestyle of this person.

I admire:

What did you say? Can you see yourself living that way? If so, then you need to begin to envision it. If your brain tends to focus on thoughts of financial insecurity and stress, you will continue to live an insecure and stressful lifestyle. This is the "power of attraction" philosophy made famous by that self-help book, *The Secret*. Like attracts like, and you have to see something before it can happen. Of course, not every dream comes true. But dreams are how change begins. Think of the part of that other person's life that you envy again. What would it look like in your life if it were realistic? Can you mold that reality into a vision of your own? Can you make that vision seem possible in the next three months? Maybe the space you are living in needs some new paint or the things you have are cluttering up your place. Maybe the fact that that person takes endless dance classes is inspiring you to join that free Tai Chi community session in the park down the street. The very thing you want may be within reach, if you can mold it to fit the parameters of your new frugal lifestyle. And, with frugality comes freedom to do as you please. So don't limit your dreams.

However, there is another possibility. Perhaps the very thing you envy (like endless spending power) is so detrimental to your growth that you need to completely change your way of thinking. I remember back around 2007 I had a friend who used to smoke cigarettes, but one day she simply quit for good. She had smoked for what I think was approximately ten years and she smoked quite regularly throughout the day. She told me that a book had made her change the way she thought about cigarettes. It was all about the reconditioning of her mind to believe that cigarettes were not pleasurable, but actually were harmful and disgusting. By the end of the book, her brain was rewired to no longer accept the concept that cigarettes equaled pleasure, and just like that, she no longer desired them. I do not mean to belittle the difficulty that many people experience when quitting smoking, but I am asking you to think in a similar way as my friend did with cigarettes. Except in your case, you aren't fighting cigarettes; you're learning to recognize your poor financial habits and dangerous financial desires. You health and your future depend on it. If you can condition your brain to realize that most urges for a shopping spree are built on a false pretense ingrained in each person by capitalism, then you won't equate shopping with pleasure any more. Need to wind-down after work? Don't stop at TJ-Maxx on the way home. Go for a walk with your dog instead. Heading out of town for the weekend? You don't need that new dress or shirt for the trip. Make due with what you have and enjoy an extra dinner out while you are traveling. You may need to re-think your consumerism. It is most likely hurting you.

Long-Term Benefits

Back in 2006, I was living in New York City and one weekend I went to visit my friend Susan in Cambridge, Massachusetts. Susan is a lawyer and by age thirty had done very well for herself. She owned a three-floor condominium on a beautiful side-street in a posh neighborhood. She lived only five minutes from the T and within walking distance to the Charles River and a Whole Foods supermarket. When I looked around at Susan's new home, I felt envy. But I also saw the results of hard work and a long-term goal. I was inspired. At the time, I was enrolled in my Ph.D. program but I knew that my future degree in history was not as monetarily valuable as her law degree. Yet I did see the financial independence that her home represented. It made an impression.

When I graduated in 2013, the job market was so poor that my prospects were rather slim.

After a hearty attempt to find a tenure-track position, I changed direction and became a high school teacher at an independent school. The pay was similar to that of a college professor and the job was far more secure. Besides, I had my goal in mind. I wanted my own home. Not a house, but a small condo. I didn't need Susan's magazine-perfect Cambridge dream home, but a simple place to call my own would suffice. As I mentioned in the previous chapter, I finally achieved this goal. But not without making the financial choices that made this dream a reality. This included living with my parents, saving a significant portion of my income, making sure I stayed out of debt, and sticking to my budget while searching for a home instead of being lured toward a property that was attractive but more expensive.

Security

Planning for your future doesn't have to be difficult, but it does provide you with the feeling of security. Think about what it would take for you to feel secure. I'd like you to do one last exercise. This is a long-term goal exercise. It is necessarily vague as it will result in a contract between you and your conscience. Answer the following questions and be as specific as you can.

What kind of place would you like to live in five years from now? How many bedrooms do you really need? Would you like to rent or buy? What would your ideal rent or mortgage be?	
How much savings would you like to put away every month? Is it a fixed amount or a percentage of your income? When will you be able to start saving this much?	
What extra things would you like to be able to do in your life? Travel? Get another degree? What is a reasonable annual budget for these extra things?	
What can you do in the next month to begin working toward your goal?	
What can you do in the next year to begin working on your goal?	

The future isn't so scary if you have a picture in mind of what it could look like. Reevaluating your needs and desires, focusing on the goals that really matter, and taking real steps towards that future are all actions that will enable you to sleep better at night. Financial health is a lifelong process. It is like exercise. You will always need to fine tune your strategy and learn new ways to improve. But each step you take will make you feel better. Trust me, you can live with less and be very happy. And as you grow and feel like you are more comfortable, then you will feel like you have more.

Chapter 5: Case Studies

Less is More:
Dominic, John and Carlos Peron

Dominic Peron is in his forties and he has two young sons, John and Carlos. The three of them currently live in Homestead, FL, just outside of Miami. This area can be quite expensive and I chose to include them here because their frugal ways are an inspiration to any family. The Peron's are proof that one adult and two children can live in a one bedroom condominium. They are used to the crowded space, and to Dominic, the financial freedom is well worth it.

Dominic and I bonded as friends over our mutual love for saving and I have a lot of respect for the way he is raising his boys. He's the only parent I know who doesn't believe that having children is expensive. But I know his lifestyle takes the vigilance and patience of a saint because he is up against the media and their continuous attempts to make his kids believe that it's okay to want more than they need. As Dominic explains: "I've debunked the idea that *kids are expensive.* If you train your kids from infancy to be spenders, to wear $50 Nike shoes, then the kids will follow suit. Additionally, you don't need to give kids their own rooms, society tells us so, but this isn't the case. If you watch the TV show

House Hunters, and the couple has two kids, the realtor will say: 'Of course you need three bedrooms.' They're selling you on this idea before you even thought about it yourself."

Yet for Dominic, as a father and also as a Christian, saving money is more than just ignoring the media, it is also a matter of ethics and responsibility. He comes from a family of spenders, so it's a wonder how he emerged as such a frugal person.

He explained his financial philosophy in this way: "Throughout my entire life, I have been influenced by the Bible. It talks about how the person who owes is enslaved to the debtee. When I was younger, I remember my parents used to have parties with other adults, and as a child, I would observe those gatherings and listen to the conversations that people had. I would notice that many of their conversations were about finances. And I heard a lot of complaining; they didn't have enough for this or that. And I thought, it seems like everyone had this problem: young and old, single and married, black and white. And this idea of indulgence, entitlement, and 'I deserve' or 'I need' didn't sit well with me. So I thought to myself, I feel just as content having as not having. Having things doesn't change me fundamentally on the inside. Over many years of having this outlook on life, I felt less weight on my shoulders the less I had. With less space and things I would have less cleaning, less broken things, and less clutter. With less responsibility over material goods, I could focus on the things that matter. This was freeing for me. I could sleep at night. My mind wasn't filled with materialism and consumerism. And if I did purchase something, I felt a short high after making that purchase. But life continues whether you have the new car or not. You still brush your teeth. You still study. The benefits of my choices are clearer now than ever because I can say that I became 100% debt free by the age of thirty nine: I have no mortgage, student loan payments, or credit card debt. When I was a teenager, I had a life goal that by the time I was 40, I wanted to be completely debt free. And it came at age 39. I feel like I almost won the lottery."

Dominic continued by sharing his thoughts about what the next stage of life will bring: "And now I'm starting this new phase of debt-free life, but with the same philosophy. I'm not going to deprive myself of every last thing, but I feel freer because I have less. And I feel pity for those who have to justify themselves by saying what they have rather than saying who they are. I don't have Facebook or Twitter. My world doesn't revolve around what's on the news. And because of this, I can focus on my two real responsibilities, my kids. I believe that debt makes you a slave. Because whoever you owe, they are the master and you are the slave."

Dominic models this lifestyle every day for John and Carlos: "As a family we don't go out to eat often. We eat mostly at home. For example, my kids like chicken nuggets from a fast-food restaurant and they have a special on Mondays: six nuggets for

$0.99. So we go on Mondays after school. Also, I do not include myself in the meal. The food is for them, not for me. I will eat whatever they can't finish, but before we go out anywhere, I make sure we eat before we leave the house. When you smell fast food while you're out, you will make a financial and a health mistake. By eating before we go out, we are less likely to be tempted by the advertisements for food. This practice has become habitual for us, and I feel like I'm teaching my kids good habits that they will continue in adulthood."

Regarding takeout food, Dominic and his sons follow a few simple rules. "Now and then we will eat pizza, but we'll buy it from a place that advertises 50% off specials. The kids know, if there's no special, don't even ask. And I always pick up the pizza so that I don't have tip the delivery person. When they ask if I'd like to add on bread sticks or a dessert, I always decline."

Dominic has received a lot of criticism about his choices and the way he is financially educating his sons. But he stands firm by his decisions and I applaud him. "Besides," he says, "criticism doesn't affect me at all. It honestly doesn't phase me. Other people don't live my life; they don't pay my bills and they aren't responsible for these two little boys. I'm focused on them, and I do what I need to do for them." For you to begin to live frugally, you will need to tune out criticism and just know in your hearts that it's better to live with less.

Dominic is separated from his children's mother. During and after their marriage, they continue to have amicable ways of solving their financial differences, as she would spend money more liberally than he would. Having separate bank accounts was another tip Dominic suggested for couples who have different spending habits. I agree with him. While I'm not married, I have lived with various partners and have always had my own account. It's always better to "pay yourself first" as my mother would say. Save your own money, handle your own bills. Too many people fight over money and most of that can be prevented through some honest conversations about spending and saving.

I asked Dominic what financial mistakes he has made in his life and what he learned from them. His answer was quick and it was obvious that he was keenly aware of this situation and had thought a lot about it.

"Oh yes. I beat myself up over this for years and I know I'm not perfect, but this was my achilles heel. I had a Toyota Camry. One day I was bored and upset, and so I thought I'd like to buy a Nissan Altima. I went to a dealership, bought the car and it was the only time I had ever been sold on something. I was convinced by the salesman to buy the car. I knew I didn't want it, but I was grieving, and suffering on a personal level."

Dominic's impulse buy was emotionally motivated, and it began a string of poor financial decisions. In fact, buying a car or a home should never be entered into lightly. These are among the largest purchases you will make in your life. So making a mistake can have some dire consequences.

"I bought that Altima, but it wasn't the one I wanted. So I turned it in for the one I really wanted. But then the car payment freaked me out, so I returned it, and I settled for another car that I didn't want once again. Then I took the third car back and got the car that I have now. It was painful and emotional. I don't know how much I lost in those deals; I probably lost $10,000. When this car was finally paid off in December 2015, I finally felt like I could begin to measure my steps toward the future. I thought for years, why did I fall into that trap? Perhaps I made that financial mistake so that one day in the future I wouldn't make another one."

Many people see a car as something more than what it really is, which is a mode of transportation. If you need a car in your life, see it as just that, a means to get from point A to point B. A car needn't be pretty, or a sign of your status or personality. It needs to be functional and suitable to your needs. Also, you should plan to have your car until the day it dies. The longer you own a vehicle, the less expensive it really is. Currently I am on year five with my Honda Fit, and I have 95,000 miles on it. I expect that I will own it for another five years or until it reaches at least 200,000 miles. If I can make my car last that long, the car will only have cost me $1,700 per year. If I traded it in now, and received $6,000 for the trade in, then the car has cost me $2,200 per year. It already has a few dents in it and it is not the most attractive or comfortable car in the world. But it works well, has great AC (a plus when you live in Florida) and gets good gas mileage. So if driving and owning a vehicle is mandatory for your life, then choose wisely and don't make an impulse buy. In fact, as I mentioned in an earlier chapter, I overpaid because while I bought the right car, I didn't negotiate the price and the dealer pulled one over on me between the initial offer and the signing. I'm wiser now that this happened, but as Dominic and I both know, these are expensive lessons to learn. It cost me $3,000 and him at least $10,000.

While I am not religious at all, I found Dominic's reference to the Bible to be good advice for all, regardless of your beliefs. As he said: "The Book of Ecclesiastes in the Bible talks about how in the grand scheme of things, there is a time for everything. A time to reap, a time to sow, a time for war, etc. My philosophy of money is born out of this philosophy of life. Everything is temporary; it shall pass. Do what you can and make something count for good. Leave that legacy for your children, because after you pass away, you leave that for them. It's important not to get caught up in the hype, the bad news, or keeping up with the neighbors. You're responsible for your own actions in life. You won't be judged for anyone else's words, actions, or deeds." This is sound advice for anyone. In order to live a life that is calm and makes you sleep with ease each night, you need to do what suits you and you alone.

I also had fun talking to John and Carlos about this book and the lessons that their dad taught them. While they each approach money in their own way, both boys think critically about saving, even at their young age. John only buys things that he actually needs and will use many times. Dominic's youngest son, Carlos handles his savings in a different way. He likes to have a cushion that makes him comfortable, and sees any amount over that as extra that he can spend on anything that he wants. Both boys count their money regularly and always know how much they have. I think they're both well-trained for a life of moderate living.

The Takeaway:
- Debt makes you a slave
- Have less stuff
- Eat before you leave the house
- Teach your kids to be financially responsible
- Couples should have separate bank accounts
- Shut out the media and don't listen to criticism
- Don't let emotions or other people influence you when making large purchases
- Learn from your financial mistakes

Thriving in New Jersey: Beth Austone

Beth and I met in graduate school in New York City. We were both working on our Ph.Ds and her research was on color in ancient Roman art. Beth is a Jersey girl at heart though, and one of the only property owners I met while in graduate school. Now in her late thirties and living in New Brunswick, NJ, she has had some of the most interesting side-jobs out of anyone I know.

Beth loves the ancient world, but makes her living as an art appraiser. And while she says that being an appraiser was by far the most lucrative of her jobs, she has made ends meet by working as a tour guide, teaching part time as an adjunct professor, and selling items on ebay and Amazon. She also moonlighted as a translator, museum guide, babysitter, pet-sitter, and tutor. "Adjuncting was by far the worst paying job, and I have since gotten out of that." Cheers to that, Beth! Full time work that is treated like part time and thus denies the worker a fair salary and benefits is exploitation.

Beth owned her own apartment, but could not rent out her apartment or sublet according to the rules of her building. So in order to stick to her budget, she cooked often and brought her own lunches and dinners to work. "I tried to eat veggies and fruits rather than the overpriced processed food.

I didn't eat out very often, but I'm a fairly small eater so when I did, I would try to take home what I could."

Sometimes, as I mentioned earlier in this book, you will find yourself unemployed. Our university adjunct faculty experienced massive layoffs in the late 2000s due to budget cuts. Beth bought health insurance on an Affordable Care Act exchange and also applied for unemployment benefits in this time period. She said she "couldn't believe it, but it helped." Of course it did, and our social safety nets are there for everyone because you never know what may happen in life.

When I asked Beth if she thought it was expensive to live in New York City, I knew that as a Jersey girl, she'd say yes. In fact, she said, "damn yes." In her own words: "I even selected a school in New Jersey so that I didn't have to reside in New York." But Beth had some great advice for anyone looking to live in a costly urban environment. "Make friends, and lots of them fast. Stop going out to the bars! Don't smoke either, it makes it harder to find a place to live and it cuts down on your livelihood. Take up a hobby and fiercely practice it. Be it knitting, running a marathon, or learning to brew your own beer." I agree with this, hobbies help us save money and give us a better sense of well-being.

The Takeaway:
- Take different jobs and ditch the ones that don't pay well
- Cook your own food

- Don't be ashamed to ask for help from the government
- Don't smoke or waste your money at a bar
- Practice a hobby

The King of Queens: Bryan Joon

First, a disclaimer: I'm related to Bryan. He's my younger cousin. He is a social worker by day and an R&B singer by night. Download his music or check out one of his shows when you're in New York, you won't be disappointed! Okay, the plug for my awesome favorite baby cousin is over. On to the financial advice!

Bryan is in his late twenties and lives in Jackson Heights, the neighborhood in Queens that unquestionably has the best food in all of New York City. It also used to be one of the most affordable neighborhoods in the borough, but it's seen a lot of "development" lately and like any nice place in New York City, its current residents are already getting priced out.

Bryan's job as a social worker uses a lot of his energy and is his primary source of income. But he has worked a number of different positions over the last ten years including working phones for telemarketing, being an eighth grade teacher, adjuncting as a sociology professor, and being a child welfare therapist. Currently he works on a team dedicated to increasing the use of PrEP, a pill that can prevent the contraction of new HIV infections. So I like to say that by day, Bryan is saving the world as a social worker and by night, he is making it more beautiful as an R&B singer.

To get by, Bryan quickly learned the ropes of NYC living. His advice: "Don't eat a lot of food. I only eat two meals a day. Cook if you can and save the food. Never eat in Manhattan; eat in Queens because it's cheaper." For his utilities, he had some success calling his electric company to get the cheapest possible electric bill. He also doesn't have a home phone, which saves him some money each month. Bryan tries not to take cabs or Uber home at night, but as every new yorker knows, sometimes this is your only option. A ride from Manhattan to the outer boroughs can cost upwards of $40 one way, which he factors in on top of his monthly transportation allowance of $116.50 for a metrocard. Bryan has managed to travel while living frugally. He earns points on his credit card and uses the rewards to fund his trips.

I agree with this strategy, and would add that the hotel points can be more economical than airline points. For example, my current points plan with Starwood hotels gives me a hotel room valued at $150/night for 3,000 points, which equals $3,000 of spending. But my Delta Airlines card gives me a domestic flight for 50,000 points! So the hotel points are by far the better deal for me because I would have to spend $50,000 to earn a $400 domestic flight.

I asked Bryan if he thought it was expensive to live in NYC. Here's what he said: "NYC is getting crazy. I'm okay for now, but the rents and housing prices keep going up. This is bad for me to say, but I almost hope there's another bubble burst because I don't know how we're going to be able to sustain these price increases. I stay here because it's home. I probably will move to Jersey or Long Island or upstate New York later in life, and I want to retire in Las Vegas because it's very cheap. But I definitely can't stay in New York City when I'm old."

I think that if you can manage to own an apartment for decades in New York, it's an ideal place to retire because you do not need a car and you have access to excellent cultural and medical facilities. But for those who cannot own an apartment, then yes, it's a near impossibility to stay in New York City for a long period of time. Even owning in that city is financially challenging as many buildings have monthly fees in excess of $800.

Bryan was very direct in his tips for anyone considering moving to NYC:
1. Get a roommate
2. Do your research. Do not pay a crazy amount of money for an "up and coming" neighborhood
3. Don't live in Manhattan
4. Pregame (drink at your apartment before going out with friends)

5. Find good credit cards with cash back or points
6. Don't have pets or kids until you make good money.

I agree with all of Bryan's advice. As someone who owned two dogs in New York, I can attest to number six. Factoring in the care for a pet, even a cat, can be tough. It's far easier to live carefree. As for having a child, sometimes it's not a planned option. But if you can wait, then do so! If you cannot wait, then be sure to read the first case study.

The Takeaway:
- Cook your own food
- Don't eat or live in an expensive neighborhood
- Use points for travel
- Live with roommates
- Know that pets and kids can be pricey

Czech Yourself:
Kristýna Brožková

At thirty-two, Kristýna is a veteran New Yorker. I met her when she first came to the city from the Czech Republic in 2010 as a guest who rented my couch in Astoria, Queens via Airbnb. Born in the city of České Budějovice, Kristýna, or Kiki as we know her, has made her way in New York City better than anyone I know. Her lowest annual income in New York was $12,000 and her highest was $30,000. What's her secret? She is a master at forming good relationships with people.

In the Czech Republic, Kiki worked as a copywriter, factory worker, and project manager. She says that this last position was the most lucrative as she was paid an above-average salary and loved her colleagues at the local university. But the job consisted mostly of paperwork and felt unsatisfying to her. In New York City, Kiki found her niche taking care of children. She has earned as little as $15 per hour and as much as $3,000 per month for this work. She calls this the most beneficial job that she has ever had. The salary is quite competitive, although she admits that she goes three months per year without any income when the family for whom she works goes on vacation. But she says that working with children satisfies her "on so many levels whereas money does not." Yet one needs money to get by, so how has she managed?

Kiki is an expert roommate and I can attest to this. As she puts it: "I've lived in shared apartments since I started college in 2003. I was always subletting someone else's place and I had a knack for finding very nice sublets and shared apartments. For me it's not only about saving money, but also enjoying the shared space and mutual interactions with roommates." This habit has helped her throughout the years. "Just last year when I was away for a while, I allowed my roommates offer my room to their friends for some money. It helped both them and me."

When we met, Kiki rented my couch through Airbnb and then decided to continue renting my couch for the better part of a year. She was a model roommate and understood the value in shared living. For example, she and I have enjoyed so many wonderful shared meals. It's one of the best parts of having a great roommate. In order to save money, Kiki advocates cooking at home as it is both economical and also much healthier. In NYC, she has some advice for those who like to eat out though: "Eating out is doable mostly during lunch because of the specials. But going out to dinner could cost you the same amount as cooking four dinners at home." One thing I remember about Kiki's stay is that while she was working at a restaurant, she would bring home delicious meals for us to share. Working in a restaurant is lucrative, but it also reduces your grocery bill. So if you're looking for a second or third job, look around your neighborhood and see if you can pick up a few shifts at a place where you'd like to eat regularly.

Kristyna also has some great advice about where to go grocery shopping, because this can make a difference between staying on budget or breaking the bank: "I usually try to do big grocery shopping for the basics in the discount supermarkets like Costco and then I get the fresh items like produce and milk in the local stores during the week. I also try to follow the daily/weekly sales and special offers. The important thing is to use groceries wisely;

don't over buy and don't waste anything. All leftovers are usable for another dish. This saves both money and the environment."

As a Czech citizen, health insurance in the US has been difficult. Kiki tries to get all of her health care needs taken care of in the Czech Republic when she is there, because she only has travel insurance here in the US, and that only covers emergencies. As a testament to my theory about how making relationships is the key to Kiki's success in New York, when she broke a tooth she fixed it by crowdsourcing. "I ask friends for help when needed, and luckily for me, it has always somehow worked. With the tooth, it turned out that my cousin's close friend is a dentist and he was nice enough to fix my tooth at cost, which was about $120 for materials. So yes, I would say that my frugal living is only possible because of nice people around me. And maybe it's also due to me believing that people are nice, altruistic and that they are always happy to help."

Like anyone living abroad, Kiki has to factor plane tickets home into her annual budget. These cost her approximately $850, which when added to her monthly ground transportation needs, equals a total monthly transportation cost of approximately $200. This is a steep increase from just one metro-card, so it's good that she's a savvy saver in other ways. It does limit her livelihood though; she admits that traveling in the US or to any place other than home is really not an option for her right now.

Kristýna believes that housing is the most expensive thing in NYC, and has always cut her costs by sharing apartments with multiple people. But it's worth it. As she says, "You gotta love it here, otherwise it's pointless to stay. For me as a single girl in her 30s, there is no place like New York. I don't feel as fulfilled anywhere else. For the single, liberal, open minded, and adventurous person, New York City is simply the best place." She does admit that once she finds a partner and has a family, she will probably move elsewhere, as many people do. "While I can easily imagine having children in the city, I think I'd prefer to live elsewhere after I have a family. I am simply assuming that the role of mother would fulfill me enough to manage anywhere else."

For someone who is on their own and loves to have a daily life that is full of diversity rather than monotony, then living in New York is great. Some people choose to spend an entire lifetime there, and for good reason. So if you are going to move to New York, or are just thinking about adjusting your budget so that you can stay there, Kiki has some advice for you: "Choose a good place to stay. You will have to work a lot and during your free time, you may find yourself too tired to explore the city. So live in a neighborhood that you will love to hang out in. And try to live as close to the subway as possible so that you can get anywhere easily. And when you need stuff, use Craigslist! People give many things away for free all the time on that website because in New York, people are always moving in or moving out!"

I can concur with Kiki's advice. We loved living in Astoria together because even if we had a lazy day off in the neighborhood, we had plenty to do and see and never felt like we were missing out. Plus, we had easy access to LaGuardia Airport, Harlem, the rest of Queens, and midtown Manhattan right from the train and busses in our neighborhood. And I think the only piece of furniture I actually bought from a store in New York was my mattress. Everything else was found on the curb, discovered on Craigslist, home-made, or handed down to me. And I sold so much on Craigslist. I know there are horror stories, but as Kiki said, "Be careful when dealing with strangers, but don't worry too much. Most New Yorkers are normal people and are as nice as you are!"

The Takeaway:

- Make friends and help each other
- Do what you love
- Live with multiple people
- Cook
- Love where you live; it eases the pain of not being able to travel
- Use Craigslist, not Amazon

Living Globally: Greta Redding

Greta and I have known each other since 1995. She is thirty nine and has been a renter in New York City, San Francisco, Istanbul, Berlin, Stockholm, and Buenos Aires. She is perhaps the most brave, outgoing, risk taker I know. She worked in the tech sector and has earned salaries that range from $20,000 to $135,000 per year. When Greta was living with family in New Jersey and working in New York, she used a temp agency to find work between acting gigs. After that, she moved into community management and trust/safety operations for various online communities. She built her career from the ground up and while I'm super proud of Greta, I also know it wasn't an easy road for her.

To travel around the world, Greta volunteered and later worked for a major tech start-up, living in a number of their collective houses for staff. This taught her to be a stellar roommate and travel companion. Therefore, finding affordable housing outside of these collectives was natural for her. She often lived with several people in affordable neighborhoods. This strategy is key for anyone on a budget looking to move to a big city for the first time. For example, if you're dreaming about New York, forget about Williamsburg or the West Village. Just forget it. Don't even look. Get your head out of the clouds and live somewhere you can afford.

As for food, Greta agrees with everyone else that cooking for yourself is the way to go. "Try to keep dining out to a minimum and when you do, don't drink alcohol." However, Greta doesn't skimp when it comes to good quality groceries and knows where she can buy the best produce at a good price. "I like organic and local, so I tend to go to farmer's markets and only buy what I need. Fortunately I don't have a family to feed, but I do like to share!" As for groceries, Greta avoids processed foods and relies on bulk foods like rice that tend to be cheaper. "A bag of rice will last you longer than a few microwavable meals that include rice in them. When in doubt, go for high protein bulk. There's a reason so many people choose lentils over ramen!"

Greta didn't always cook her own food, but she's always managed to eat very healthy food nonetheless. And this has helped her stay healthy even if her job didn't provide health insurance. To get by without seeing a doctor, Greta took vitamins and used herbal remedies. I remember getting really sick once when I was uninsured, and Greta taught me about using a neti pot and the merits of oregano oil. Both worked like a charm. There are so many websites and books that explain herbal remedies for almost every illness, so I won't bother to go into them here. But know that for most colds, some infections, mild digestion issues, and many other ailments, there are cheap remedies using stuff that you probably already have in your kitchen. If you need to see a doctor, find a local clinic that provides services for low income people. In New York there is a great clinic geared for LGBTQ people called the Callen Lorde Center. Greta swears by the wonderful services provided by Planned Parenthood: "Planned Parenthood was a godsend in my twenties. They covered birth control, PAP and annual exams, and STI tests. I don't know what I would have done without them."

As for transportation, Greta estimates spending approximately $150 a month on gas for her scooter in San Francisco and for taxi services like Lyft or Uber. For many urban dwellers, owning a car is too expensive and public transportation can also be slow and costly. So depending on where you live, learning to drive a scooter and supplementing this with a car service can cost approximately the same as buying an expensive monthly public transit pass. And if you have a car, Greta says, "figure out the best way to prevent yourself from getting parking tickets. There's nothing worse than factoring the price of tickets into your transportation budget!"

Overall, Greta has some great tips for those about to embark on their new urban life: "Have money saved up in advance and be very careful about your spending. Check the local markets right away so that you're not ordering takeout during your first few weeks. And as always, have roommates so that your rent is not outrageous."

The Takeaway:
- Live in an affordable neighborhood and have more than one roommate

- Don't eat out a lot and if you do, don't drink alcohol
- Buy in bulk and learn to cook foods like lentils which are very healthy and not expensive
- Become well-versed in herbal and other natural remedies when you can't afford to go to the doctor
- Go to low-cost health clinics for basic health-care needs

The Manhattanite Survivalist: Maleeha K.

Maleeha and I met during our senior year at Smith College. She came to Smith from Lahore, Pakistan and after Smith, she moved to New York City to pursue a career on Wall Street. Maleeha can be described as someone with perseverance, logic, heart, and honesty. During the recession, she was laid off and found herself unemployed for approximately one year. But because Maleeha has the aforementioned qualities, she used her year to her benefit as a time to travel and seek new experiences. She called it her "Eat, Pray, Love" year and through it all, she didn't let her expensive midtown apartment hold her back. Ensuring that she could enjoy her precious free time, she sublet it to another renter so that she could better experience life on her budget. As a Wall Street veteran, Maleeha made more money over the course of her career than most people surveyed here, but I include her because of her lessons on how to survive unemployment.

Being laid off was an emotional roller coaster for Maleeha as it is for most people. I remember that fateful day as we decompressed in her apartment and played Punjabi dance music while the rest of Manhattan continued chipping away at their office jobs. Earlier that morning, she was let go. The shock is a tough one to get over, but being logical in her survival tactics helped her get through. Maleeha's first logical decision (besides dancing on the day that she was laid off) was to sublet her apartment. As she said, "I rented my apartment for a year. It started out as an arrangement that would last a few months, but in the end, the tenant took it for a year. At first I rented another studio apartment, but after three months, I decided that I couldn't afford it and spent the remainder of the year with friends." Like Kiki, having a good social network is an essential strategy for surviving any financial crisis. Your friends not only will provide shelter and food, but chances are, they will also lead you toward your next opportunity.

Regarding food and going out, Maleeha recommends discount grocery stores like Trader Joe's. Sometimes you will pay a premium if you shop in smaller, local markets. I remember in Queens, the Key Food supermarket was actually quite expensive, while another supermarket called Trade Fair was far more reasonable. You may need to travel to a different neighborhood for the best prices, so get to know your options and comparison shop. When Maleeha goes out, she doesn't like to split the bill because like Greta said, she won't consume alcohol at dinner. "If you end up splitting the tab, then it gets awkward as you realize that you're paying for something that you didn't consume." To avoid this, Maleeha suggests meeting friends for coffee and avoiding dinner all together. I would add that you should especially avoid large dinner parties at restaurants. You'll have very little control over the bill once it arrives and most restaurants in New York will not provide separate checks as they readily do in other states.

Health care is important to Maleeha and she is a bit of an expert in this department. She negotiated an exit package when she was laid off, not for money, but for health care. Additionally, she recommends knowing the rules about using your remaining Flexible Spending Account money if you have this program as part of your health insurance and you find yourself suddenly laid off. "Be in conservation mode and if you lose your job on the 5th of the month, find out if your health insurance will run out on the 15th or on the last day of that month." She also has good advice for those considering time off or a career change: "Know your current employer's healthcare options for after you leave, and learn about your future employer's healthcare options before you join their firm."

Maleeha still lives in her midtown Manhattan apartment. After being there for more than a decade, it seems increasingly more and more affordable as the rents rise around her. This is the case for many New Yorkers who stay put and find that they can't afford to move. But living in midtown Manhattan has a few financial benefits. Transportation costs are lower as most Manhattanites walk to work or school. They tend to buy "pay as you go" metrocards rather than shelling out $116 for a monthly metrocard. This a small consolation for the price of living in this exceedingly expensive borough, but no matter where you live, you may find that paying per ride is cheaper than a monthly pass. Do the math and make a wise choice for yourself. If you can't afford a monthly pass, then walking or cycling may be a better alternative. Plus, you will not need to join a gym to stay fit! An hour walking commute is no oddity in New York and while cycling can be precarious, there are more and more bike paths popping up around the city. When Maleeha needs a break from the chaos of Manhattan, she goes to visit a friend who lives outside of the city. She helps her friend with housework, childcare and cooking, and they help her by giving her a break from the city. Like Greta and Kristýna, Maleeha knows the importance of a good social network.

For recent migrants to the Big Apple, Maleeha has some wonderful advice: "Always be ready to be unemployed in this city. Anything can happen. You can be at the top of your game and still find yourself with a pink slip in your hand. Don't spend all of the money you make, no matter what you make, and be careful with the money you have, whenever you find yourself with a surplus. Savings, retirement and health insurance are all important, basic needs that you should strive to provide for yourself." Maleeha's words echo those of my mother: "Pay yourself first."

And regarding your first months in your new city, Maleeha says, "You may come to the city thinking that you have saved enough for three months of living expenses and then find yourself out of money within a month. Whatever you do, don't go into credit card debt to maintain your habits. NYC is an enticing experience, however we all cannot afford every part of it."

This banker has survived and thrived in the Big Apple for the better part of the last two decades. She survived 9/11 and a major lay off. She even has a family now, and all four of them continue to live in her one bedroom midtown apartment. Maleeha knows, as much as the others featured in these case studies, that changing your habits will help you live the life you want and accomplish the goals you set for yourself.

The Takeaway:
- Get rid of or sublet your place if you can't afford it
- Stay with friends when you need to in order to save money or for a cheap getaway
- Plan for a disaster
- Meet for coffee, not dinner
- Walk everywhere
- Make good friends
- Don't get into credit card debt

Conclusion

I hope that this book has helped you rethink your finances. As I often tell my sociology students, I probably won't teach you anything that you didn't already know, but I will teach you to think more critically about the things that you do know. I hope I have accomplished this for you.

As you've read this far, I will now give you a concise list of the key ideas so that you can keep them in your mind as you embark on your future of financial freedom.

Key Ideas from *The Envelope System*:

- Know how much you have and don't overspend. Stick to a strict budget.
- Revise your budget at least twice a year, and be sure to do this every time you get or lose a job or a new income source.
- The envelope system is good for both budgeting and saving.
- Reduce your need for personal and household goods. Less is more. The less you have, the less you'll need or want.
- The joy in shopping is a product of capitalism. Don't fall into that trap. Shopping isn't fun. It isn't therapeutic. Buy only what you really need and be judicious about your spending.

- Value experience over goods. You will enjoy your city or your vacation far more than the clothes you buy or the new cell phone you have.
- Seek out free things; furniture, experiences, clothing, and even food and lodging can all be found for free or close-to-free.
- Work multiple jobs, but don't keep the ones that waste your time for little pay. Keep the ones that provide decent pay for the effort and time you put in and prioritize the ones that are fulfilling over the jobs that seem menial to you.
- Cobble together various ways of earning money. Sell things, trade things, or teach people. You have valuable goods and skills that can help you get by.
- Credit cards are evil. Hide them in your closet and only use them when you really need to.
- Pets and children can be expensive. Think and try to plan ahead as best as possible.
- Set goals for yourself and clearly delineate a path that leads you to your goal.
- Living frugally will mean you are living more responsibly, but with greater emotional health and personal freedom. Embrace the new, frugal you!

I know that there are aspects of life that this book left out. I chose brevity in the hopes that you would actually read it in its entirety. If you would like to reach out with questions or comments, I'm easy to find on Facebook and welcome your message.

Overall, know that having a fixed income doesn't have to mean feeling despair or stress over your finances. Anyone can live well on a lower income, they just have to be really crafty about it. I know it's frustrating, and you might feel overwhelmed or defeated now. But hang in there. You've made the right choice by picking up this book. Hopefully you've actually done the work with a pencil and if you haven't, then go back and do it now. You'll be happy that you did. Financial knowledge is the first step to financial freedom. Best wishes, dear reader. And good luck!